HOUSES NATURAL
NATURAL HOUSES

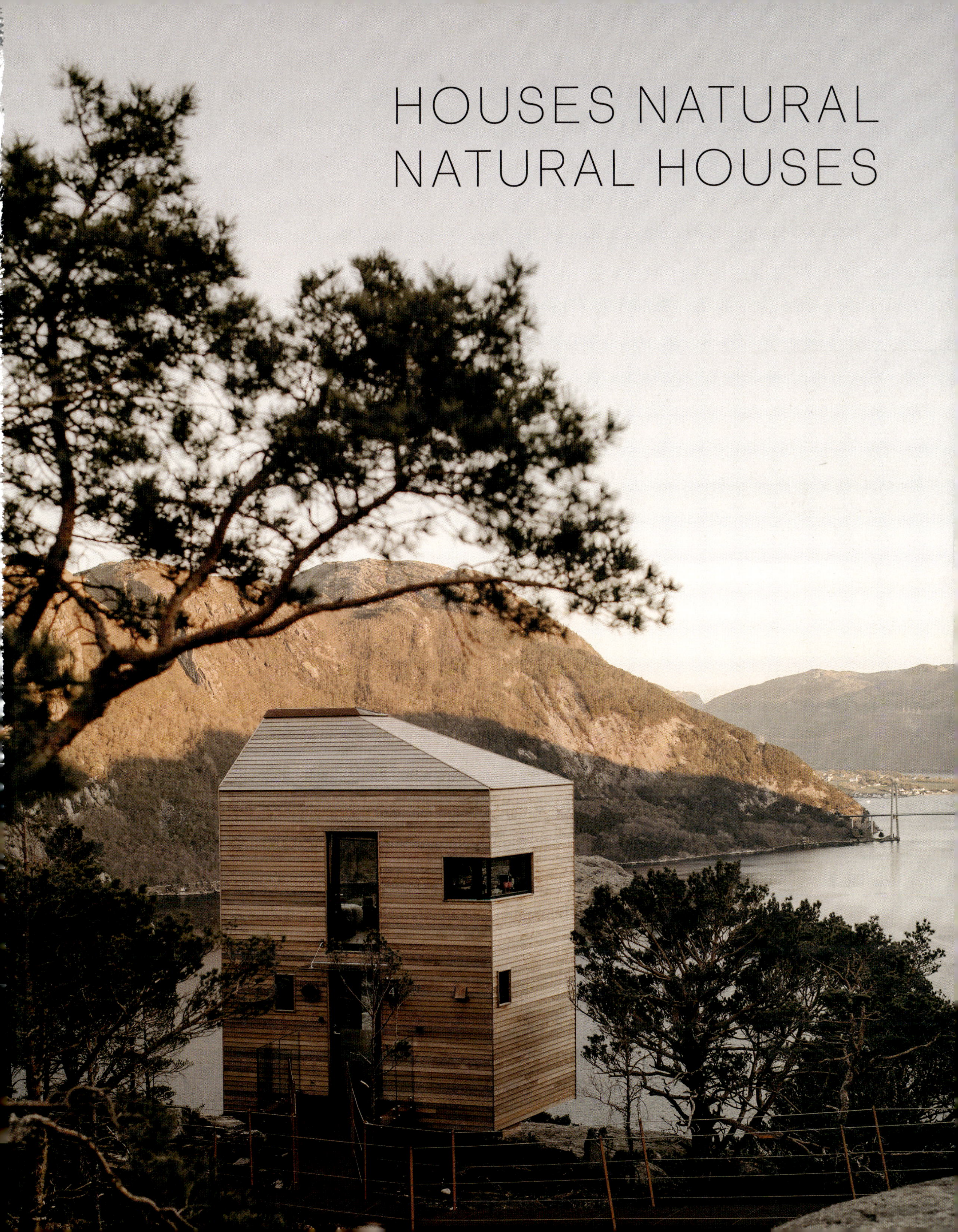

HOUSES NATURAL

homes that return to nature

NATURAL HOUSES

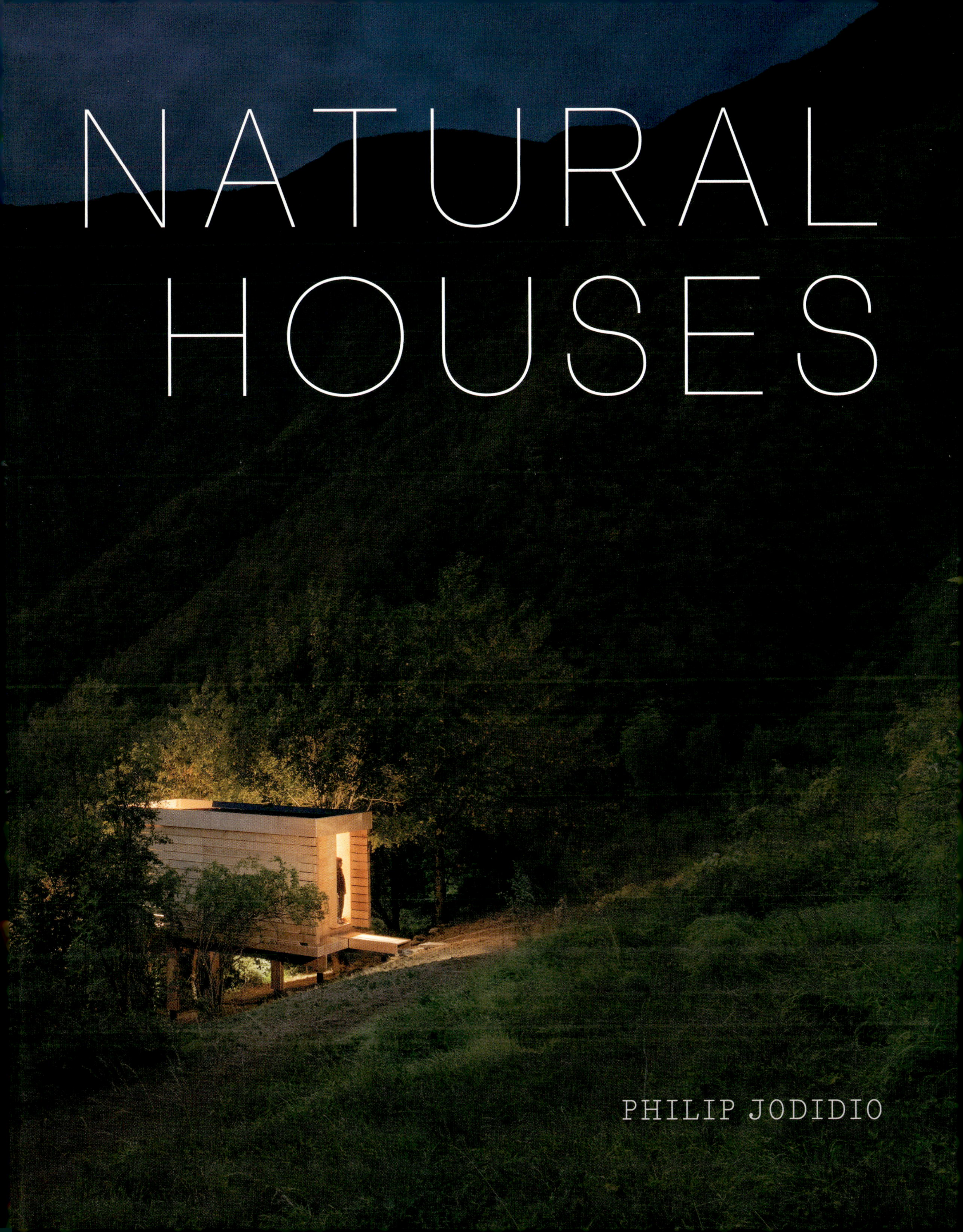

PHILIP JODIDIO

contents

(contents)

REGAINING PARADISE

In the beginning . . . a home was shelter, a place to weather a storm, or to keep out threatening animals and people. It is obvious that the earliest houses had to be created with very simple tools and locally sourced materials.

Freighters did not ply the oceans with keel loads of Zimbabwe black granite ballast, diesel-operated construction machinery, and generators didn't spew out clouds of polycyclic aromatic hydrocarbons, formaldehyde, and nitrogen oxides. Of course, there were fewer people to house at the time, but a home had to be relatively easy to get to and not too complicated to build. And so, with centuries of "progress," these basic facts of the home were gradually eroded, and technology began to permit construction in the most extreme terrains, devoid of any consideration for the natural environment. Ultimately, living in a natural setting wasn't even desirable; city living implied more and more concrete, asphalt, and of course, pollution. The allure of nature was always there nonetheless: the quest for Arcadia, even the myth of the Garden, the original unspoiled place from which we all came, it seems. Yes, *Paradise Regained* even without religious fervor was a call heard through the ages, and in many faiths and cultures. In Islam, the garden is an earthly symbol of yearning for paradise. But no need to digress into the history of religion and culture. The steamroller of modernity, indifferent to nature, laid down the paths, sprayed pollutants in the air and water, and began to kill nearly every flying, swimming, crawling thing. Then, suddenly, a desire, or even a need to return to nature, arose. At first a "gadget," a fledgling call born of Rachel Carson's *Silent Spring* (1962), began to suggest that there should be other ways to produce the goods of modern society. Over the years since then, the environmental havoc wrought by human activities during what has now been termed our very own epoch, the *Anthropocene*, has became ever more obvious with rising temperatures and waters. And so, in a conjuncture of forces that is unlikely to recede in the foreseeable future, more and more persons have been looking for ways to live with and in nature.

opposite Costa Rica Treehouse, Olson Kundig

The Call of the Wild

The fifty-one recent homes in this book were selected with a view to the different aspects of this trend. A most obvious direction is represented by the number of people who literally want to heed the call of the wild and live in forests and mountain ranges, or on a distant beach. This movement is joining with another, perhaps more fundamental search for "sustainability"—not the kind promoted by the voracious appetite of Tesla for lithium, cobalt, aluminum, plastics, and titanium, but something again more down-to-earth. A house with a tiny carbon footprint from inception to demolition. Wood, a renewable resource if it is responsibly harvested; stone, that other mainstay of construction for thousands of years; and even energy derived from the sun (albeit via photovoltaics made with cadmium telluride, copper indium selenide, cadmium gallium (di)selenide, copper indium gallium (di)selenide, hexafluoroethane, lead, polyvinyl fluoride, and other delights) are part of the new equation. Even accounting for the (rare) earth hunger of modern technology, the sustainable house is emerging from the depths of catastrophic pollution, emitting just a bit less carbon overall and leaving behind a smaller trail of toxic waste than the preceding generation.

And so yes, it is possible to again dare to approach nature, this time with a more respectful and less all-conquering mentality, in order to live *with and in* nature. Living with *and* in nature are not mutually exclusive, nor are they necessarily to be paired. Living with nature can imply reaching for the goals and means of sustainability even if it is in a more developed environment than the Pacific coast of Nicaragua or a remote bay on Bruny Island in Tasmania. Of course, it is recognized more and more that a remote, natural place must be protected, indeed nurtured, rather than imagining that it offers a license to unleash the entire panoply of contemporary pollutants on environments that have evolved over thousands of years. Parts of the world and some cultures clearly still seek to occupy large, luxurious spaces for small numbers of people. Architects with talent do often tend to work for the wealthy, but several projects in this book point in a different direction, toward living with less, in smaller spaces, with fewer manufactured and imported amenities. Faced with new challenges, architects, in particular younger ones and persons from different parts of the world not previously on the big map of Pritzker Prize winners, find solutions, with small budgets, with new materials, or with old materials, suddenly again fashionable. Upcycling, or creative reuse, is present, not necessarily in any politically motivated context, but because more and more people have been made aware of the catastrophic results of industrial production. Then too, recuperated wood or scrap metal (admittedly not very present in these pages) have the virtue of being inexpensive in a time of rising costs and challenged budgets. Those of us born into a world where the future seemed bright have some difficulty with the idea of learning to live with less, and yet rising populations coupled with a lack of environmental controls have all but made it inevitable that less is not only more, it *is* the future.

opposite Captain Kelly's Cottage, John Wardle

Surf's Up

A remote bay on Bruny Island (Tasmania) and an isolated beach in Nicaragua were not cited by chance—these are in fact places where houses of interest have been fashioned, or refashioned, to enter the spirit of these times, conscious of ecology, conscious of place. John Wardle, one of Australia's best-known architects, undertook the renovation and modernization of an 1840s Tasmanian cottage named after its original owner, Captain Kelly. Tasmanian oak and a courtyard offering the shelter of the leeward side of the old house are elements that make the old building new. One of the main ways to reduce the pollution and carbon footprint of architecture is to bring back to life old buildings. The use of new materials is reduced drastically, and here, the importation of materials from distant corners of the world is distinctly obviated. Instead, old bricks and wood retain the burnished finish of time in a structure that has been made anew. The young Spanish architect Dani Serrano found his corner of paradise on a beach in Nicaragua (Aposentillo, Chinandega). Using a camper he bought in Oregon that he had driven south, Serrano purchased a coastal site and installed the vehicle on stilts, adding partitions and an outdoor bath. A roof for the rainy season and hanging paper lamps for night lighting were almost all he needed to make a camper into a home. Both in terms of potential mobility and for its low use of new resources aside from the original vehicle, Serrano's Camper House is an example of how to "explore the romance of what is not needed" as he puts it. Minimal resources and space, reuse of existing materials, and a certain sense of style and openness to outdoor life make this 2022 project exemplary in many ways.

"And Not Sometimes Be Content with Less?"

Not so many years ago, a survey of recent homes would have focused only on North America, Europe, and possibly Japan. Today, largely because of the Internet, information (and interesting architecture) is found almost everywhere. With its history of major contributions to modern architecture and significant figures such as Oscar Niemeyer, Lina Bo Bardi, Paulo Mendes da Rocha, and from a younger generation, Alejandro Aravena, Latin

America is now one of the most inventive and dynamic areas of the world for contemporary architecture. Mexico, for example, home to Luis Barragán and Pedro Ramirez Vazquez, has continued to affirm its place on the world stage. In Mexico, as in other countries, a new element is the emergence of significant female architects, like Tatiana Bilbao and Frida Escobedo. In this book, the Casa Nidos (Claudia Rodríguez + Rozana Montiel, Valle de Bravo, 2021) was imagined, as its name implies, like a bird's nest. In good part suspended above the ground, collecting its rainwater and treating wastewater on-site, this residence is immersed in its natural setting, using wood and stone but also warmly colored concrete to further blend into the lush environment. The connection to nature is not only one of appearances or even environmentally conscious design, it is also a place that brings residents (back) into contact with the site, with the green environment of a world not yet flattened and devasted by asphalt and towers. A warm climate obviously makes spaces that are partially or completely open possible, perhaps one reason that new houses in Mexico are so attractive.

In Brazil, the country of Niemeyer, there has been a long tradition of creating weekend or vacation houses outside the cities in the forested environments near the Atlantic coast. One example of this type of home is the Cabana, an ongoing project by Thiago Bernardes and his family located in Paraty in the state of Rio de Janeiro. At just 1,292 square feet (120 square meters), the Cabana does not rival with the very large and modern residences that dot the coastal areas, but the glulam structure with modular panels does succeed in reconciling a dense forested setting with a certain degree of comfort. Again, the warm climate helps to make a convivial space that uses only a small generator for its electricity. "This space has awnings as the only enclosure," says the architect.

There is, of course, a world of literary influences that evoke the romance and possible inconveniences of this kind of return to nature—ranging from Daniel Defoe's *Robinson Crusoe* (1719) to Henry David Thoreau's *Walden, or Life in the Woods* (1854). Thoreau wrote,

"Most men appear never to have considered what a house is and are actually though needlessly poor all their lives because they think that they must have such a one as their neighbors have. As if one were to wear any sort of coat which the tailor might cut out for him, or gradually leaving off palm leaf hat or cap of woodchuck skin, complain of hard times because he could not afford to buy him a crown! Is it not possible to invent a house still more convenient and luxurious than we have, which yet all would admit that man could not afford to pay for. Shall we always study to obtain more of these things, and not sometimes be content with less?"

Temperature, Warmth, Color, Smell, Taste

The architect Guillermo Acuña (GAAA) designed his Casa Detif (Chiloé Island, Chile, 2021) on a sloped, forested site 621 miles (1,000 kilometers) south of Santiago. Built on stilts to preserve the natural site, and to protect from flooding and erosion, the Casa Detif was made with modular CNC panels made with locally sourced pine. Acuña pleads not only for responsible building but also for a more sensitive approach to nature, one with a heightened awareness of "temperature, warmth, color, smell, taste, hardness or softness, senses through which we relate to Nature prior to knowledge." It is certain that building with and in nature often is equivalent to completely sheltering residents from the vicissitudes of the real world. A steady year-round temperature where a lucky few can gaze from picture windows into pristine mountains and forests, always comfortable, never challenged to really feel nature. The Casa Detif is more in contact with nature than several other houses in this book, precisely because living with and in nature can be defined in many ways. Even the theoretical standards of LEED or the much trumpeted advances in off-grid living systems tend to take some factors into account while ignoring others. Complex systems of fabrication and construction generate forms of pollution and by-products that may be no less harmful than the gaseous and chemical potions of the past. One needs to get very much back to basics, as Thoreau suggested 170 years ago, to have any very substantial impact, and even that implies a vast movement toward sustainability that would inevitably engender new and unexpected

opposite Nidos House, Claudia Rodríguez + Rozana Montiel Estudio de Arquitectura

problems, much like sourcing the materials needed for the lithium-ion batteries used in electric cars.

Effectively Compostable Living

Some contemporary houses are almost entirely based on the quest for carbon for the smallest embodied carbon footprint possible. The idea of embodied carbon is relatively new, more recent than standards that measure only carbon emissions (now called operational carbon), for example. Embodied carbon is defined by the carbon dioxide (CO_2) emissions associated with materials and construction processes throughout the whole life cycle of a building or infrastructure. It includes any CO_2 created during the manufacturing of building materials (material extraction, transport to manufacturer, manufacturing), the transport of those materials to the job site, and the construction practices used.[1] An interesting initiative in this respect is the Block House (Somerset, UK, 2021) designed by Material Cultures (London). Built with locally sourced timber and wood-fiber insulation, as well as hempcrete, the 969-square-foot (90-square-meter) house sits on flint foundations. Other materials used in the house such as clay-based paints were selected so that the entire house is "effectively compostable," addressing a very significant albeit mostly hidden aspect of the pollution produced by architecture—the waste materials generated at demolition. Set on the grounds of an old estate, the Block House is to some extent in a natural setting, but it is as close to being one with nature as possible—ashes to ashes as it were.

Another rather academic or technical application of the quest for the natural home is illustrated by the self-built 129-square-foot (12-square-meter) Hermitage (Val Trebbia, Italy, 2021) from LLABB (Genoa). Plywood surfaces, wooden pillars set in the sandstone of the site, a composting toilet, and an inherent modesty make the Hermitage another example of doing more with less, perhaps one of the quickest and most efficient routes to reducing pollution. In this instance, the small house is both in and with nature, a remote place to contemplate or dream, a structure that could be easily removed, or that might return almost entirely to the earth if it were left in place. Another example of "compostable" architecture.

From Ochoalcubo to Kawaguchiko

All of this is not to say that there are no longer spectacular modern houses being built in largely natural settings. The Casa Ochoalcubo (Los Vilos, Coquimbo Region, Chile, 2021) by Max Núñez is part of a high-profile series of oceanside residences by figures such as the Pritzker Prize–winners Alejandro Aravena (Elemental) and Ryue Nishizawa (SANAA). The very modern house with curving panoramic views of the Pacific was built in sand dunes and finds its shape inspired by nature in the form of bivalve mollusks. The architects are aware of the significance of local biodiversity, and it may well be that individual projects like this one have a much lighter impact than would denser and larger habitations. Nature is all around this house, and it is made to take in the breathtaking spectacle. A world away in terms of both geography and culture, the Tokyo architect Shinichi Ogawa designed the Lakeside House (Yamanashi, Japan, 2015). Built on the shore of Lake Kawaguchiko near Mount Fuji, this house assumes fully minimalist and very modern vocabulary, the single thin, 98-foot-long (30-meter) steel and glass volume is situated and designed to take in the beauty of the landscape and lake. The architect protected trees on the site but otherwise opted for a kind of refined modernism, Mies by the lake as it were. In this place, the shimmering light reflected from the lake inhabits the house, an idea that is familiar to the Japanese, who see expression of nature not only in views but also in the way the breeze blows through, and the sun penetrates a building. Ogawa does not make a documented case for the ecological credentials of the Lakeside House, but it was quite obviously conceived with and in nature.

Windows on the War

Indeed, many parts of the world see the construction of solid, comfortable homes in natural settings. In at least one case in this book, this configuration is far less tranquil than images might make it seem. The

1 https://www.carboncure.com/concrete-corner/what-is-embodied-carbon, accessed May 29, 2023.

opposite Casa Detif, Guillermo Acuña Arquitectos Asociados (GAAA)

House Among the Pines by ArchObraz was completed in 2022 in Dnipro, Ukraine, not far from the war zone. The architect carefully considered the impact of the structure on the forest environment and sought to make as much use of passive energy strategies as possible. A heat pump is used for ventilation, air-conditioning, and heating, as well as hot water. The external cladding is in locally sourced metal and wood.

Perhaps even more touching and significant than the story of this house is the expression of Oleksii Obraztsov, the principal architect involved, as laid out in a lengthy e-mail sent to the author on May 24, 2023. Until recently, it may have been felt that war in the old sense of the word could no longer exist, and yet, the events in Ukraine have made it clear that, sometimes, the new concern for sustainability must be set aside to deal with more urgent challenges. Giving a rare insight into the life of an architect near the front lines, Obraztsov wrote:

> *Our bureau continues to work in Dnipro. Of the fourteen architects in the team, only seven are now working because of the war. Three female architects have gone abroad. I had to temporarily suspend collaboration with four architects from the team because of economic difficulties. My wife (also an architect of ArchObraz) with our son moved to our daughter, to the Czech Republic, where she studied architecture in Prague before the war.*
>
> *Our team and I personally participate in discussions about the future reconstruction of the country. Festivals, competitions, forums, dialogues with*

foreign partners, discussions and self-education are all a common powerful movement towards rethinking life and seeing a common future in our rather diverse cities of a multinational country. . . . In 2023, I joined the competition committee of the Union of Architects. Unfortunately, the current public procurement system involves finding an architectural project executor through a tender, based on the lowest possible cost of the work! This is a real tragedy, because you can only get a public contract by offering a lower cost or through the "corruption window." It is important to change this practice of obtaining orders. At the same time, it is necessary to change the design principles based on post-Soviet standards in the context of the country's European integration. Civil society needs to change, but there was already a crisis of administration before the war. . . . Discussions about the future of urban planning are continuing in Dnipro. As an experiment, in order to educate ourselves, our office developed a concept for the spatial development of a certain district in Dnipro; we also made a project for housing for displaced people, also in our hometown . . .

Thank you for your books, Philip! Some of them were my first textbooks. Thanks to them, I was able to get acquainted with examples of high-quality world architecture for the first time. Thank you for the opportunity to tell you a little bit about our office and life.

above House Among the Pines, ArchObraz

Becoming Part of the Forest

Another unusual house in terms of its site and architect is the House in the Forest (Rankoshi, Hokkaido, Japan, 2020) by Florian Busch. He explains that the client "brief was not for a house but for a time in and with the forest." Inspired by the form of a natural branch, the 2,476-square-foot (230-square-meter) dwelling has full-height windows at the end of each ramification, implying that in a way the residents can sense the trees as part of their "tactile environment" and "become part of the forest." Although it was built on a concrete slab, the house is made essentially of wood and was built in an existing clearing, implying a minimum of damage to the forest itself. It is certain that every country, indeed every region has a different approach to new construction in a wilderness area. Japan is particular in that it has one of the densest urban environments in the world, along the Tokyo-Osaka corridor near the Pacific Ocean. Inland, the hilly topography has kept many areas from being paved over, and natural spaces are quite abundant. Hokkaido is less developed in general than the main island of Honshu. Rankoshi is 66 miles (106 kilometers) southwest of the city of Sapporo near ski resorts and *onsen* (hot baths), so it is a vacation place, and the town itself has only about five thousand inhabitants. A house in the forest here can certainly be considered a place to escape from Japanese urban life and to reconnect with the forest, as the architect has clearly attempted to do.

Many of the houses in this book were designed by individuals or by small architectural firms. When larger firms get involved, it is often with the hope of proving a point or developing an idea. The Glass Villa on the Lake (Lechlade, UK, 2018) is by the large Rotterdam practice Mecanoo. No small object, the villa has a floor area of 6,458 square feet (600 square meters) and is located in a luxury home development. Transparency was a guiding word for the architecture, and thus views of the lake and countryside in the Cotswolds. With its home cinema, bar, and wellness spa located below grade, the house clearly falls into the domain of luxury, although the architects underline the sustainability of the design. The strong modern and rectangular presence of the house certainly does not rhyme with the kind of "hand-made" approach of other architects and designers in natural environments, but the "Lakes by Yoo" (name of the development) are also not in a completely undisturbed setting. The need to be surrounded by nature, to be immersed in it, is expressed both by the architects and surely the clients in this instance.

opposite House in the Forest, Florian Busch Architects

Small but Perfectly Formed

Another large firm that sometimes delves into home design and small sustainable structures is Snøhetta, from Oslo. Their recent design, The Bolder (Lysefjorden, Norway, 2023), is part of a four-cabin project perched above the fjord with "natural and durable materials in earthy colors and organic textures." Untreated red cedar and concrete made with aggregate from the site are used for the buildings that sit above the ground and are off-grid in their conception. With kitchen and dining space designed by Vipp and a firm like Snøhetta at the controls, these cabins are quite luxurious by definition. The glass facades are meant to give residents the impression that they are "floating in the air" above the mountainous landscape. Perhaps more "ecological" than Mecanoo's Glass Villa, The Bolder is nonetheless an example of bringing luxury living to a natural environment, perhaps a trend that will be less popular in the future than it clearly still is. Again, without any trace of irony, it can be noted that four small structures with a small carbon footprint will not change the balance of the climate nor of the overall natural environment of the western coast of Norway, and being off-grid is certainly a way to ease the burden on shared resources. The view looks great!

There are also recognized firms and architects who specialize in design and construction in natural or wilderness environments. One of the best known of these is Tom Kundig of the Seattle practice Olson Kundig. His Costa Rica Treehouse (Santa Teresa, Costa Rica, 2017) takes us back to the Pacific coast of Central America. Built with locally harvested teak, with a photovoltaic array providing power, the three-level Treehouse is billed as "carbon positive." In the rainy season, all water needs of the house are covered by a subterranean

rain catchment system that is part of the project. Three stories high and yet light in its appearance and reality, the house was a winner of the 2022 American Institute of Architects (AIA) Housing Awards, where the jury commented, "In many ways, the home is a large solar umbrella sitting on four live edge teak logs and enclosed by porous screens." The fact that the clients are environmental activists clearly had something to do with the very nature of this design. In Kundig, they also found an architect who was prepared to listen not only to them, but to the site, to the dense growth and life of this place. Of course, an approach to nature in a contemporary house depends on many factors, but the clients often can play a significant role. Nor is it necessary for well-known architects to prove that they can bring every luxury of a city apartment to the jungle—here the balance has been respected and the result is what the AIA jury called "a masterfully simple home that elevates shelter to a poetic level."

The Costa Rica location for Kundig's Treehouse was something of an exception in his career, which has been more focused on the United States. Far from being eclipsed by architects from other parts of the world, Americans hold an unusual place in the area of environmentally conscious houses. Two very small structures that can almost be qualified as marginal demonstrate aspects of their inventiveness in this volume. Michael Quirk's Magnolia Net Zero Cabin (Nederland, Colorado, 2022) measures just 120 square feet (11 square meters) and was built with birch plywood, reused cedar shiplap siding, shou sugi ban charred pine, reused windows, a wood-burning stove, hempcrete, solar panels, reused bricks, metal panels that had been furnished as architectural samples, and certified Douglas fir framing. All these factors add up to a "net-zero" cabin that actually stores more carbon than what was used to build it. Handmade, reused, recycled materials and an understanding of energy use and the environment allow a building like this to be built for a very low budget, inspiring Quirk to suggest that his approach could be used to create affordable housing for persons otherwise excluded from having their own residence.

opposite Magnolia Net Zero Cabin, Michael Quirk Design

Ephemeral Shelter

Another interesting American project is the Joshua Tree Case Study Cabin (Joshua Tree, California, 2017) by the photographer, artist, and designer Mike Vensel. Inspiring himself from the famous Case Study Houses, which were experiments in residential architecture built between 1945 and 1964 almost entirely in California, Vensel created an off-grid cabin using lumber, light waterproof fabric, and solar panels. Priced at under $2,000 for materials, the Joshua Tree Case Study Cabin is also a take on the homes of nomadic peoples—one that the designer sees as offering potential solutions for the homeless of California. At just 208 square feet (19 square meters), the cabin offers minimal comfort that corresponds to its "less is more" approach. After a long period in which it was hoped that "modern" materials like steel and concrete could create long-lasting homes, there has been a shift to willfully ephemeral ideas that are also based on the desire to leave the smallest possible footprint, in every sense of the word. Granted, waterproof fabric and solar panels contain their list of unpleasant ingredients, but the quantities concerned are far less deleterious than what goes into the average US house—the 2021 average for new homes was 2,480 square feet (230 square meters), more than ten times the size of Vensel's experimental shelter. The climate in Joshua Tree National Park might allow this kind of shelter to be habitable for several months a year—March to May and October to November. In terms of ecology, living in temperate or warmer climates has the potential to limit carbon footprints more than places of extreme cold or heat. This seems like an obvious fact, but discussions of CO_2 emissions sometimes do not dwell on specific climates.

Nordic Engawa

A part of the world that has long built cabins and houses in natural settings is, of course, Scandinavia. The Bolder by Snøhetta has already been mentioned here, but other homes in this book are also in the Nordic countries. A first case with an amusing name is Gimme Shelter (Väddö, Sweden 2021), which is on an island in the Baltic Sea. It has two volumes, one with living or public space and the other for a bedroom. The designer

Emelie Holmberg has imagined creating such houses with a system she compares to LEGO—with plug-in modules. With some industrially produced elements, the structure can be less difficult and expensive to build. Her design draws ideas from the sliding walls (*shoji*) of Japanese houses and the in-between veranda space (*engawa*) also familiar in the same country. The result of obvious public interest in creating off-grid homes in natural settings, this project is also born of the great increase in information about architecture that is circulating on the Internet— LEGO and Japan are not the most obvious starting points for a Swedish cabin, but Holmberg is quite at ease with these points of reference. There is a hybridization afoot that is changing architecture in general, and smaller, less expensive structures are very much in that trend. The Aurora Lodge by Snorre Stinessen is in the north of Norway on the Norwegian Sea. This is essentially an A-frame house with some tweaks that give it a broader view of the water. It has a concrete floor and terraces but was built without cutting trees on the site. With materials chosen to avoid toxic substances, it succeeds in having a "positive carbon footprint," thus combining a modern appearance with a strong sense of ecology. Municipal hydroelectric power is used for the house; it apparently will go off-grid "within three to five years."

Gimme the Woods

Like Thoreau's cabin on Walden Pond, or even Le Corbusier's 144-square-foot (13.4-square-meter) Cabanon (Roquebrune-Cap-Martin, 1951), for ages architects and thinkers have echoed the longing of many simple homeowners to live in a natural setting. There was certainly a great turning away from the scenic beauty of nature as modernity swept the world. A landscape of skyscrapers was so much more thrilling than mountains and beaches. As cities became denser and often more polluted, people again began to look to nature for solace and beauty. In modern times, a house like Frank Lloyd Wright's Fallingwater (Mill Run, Pennsylvania, 1936–39) was the indication that some were already attracted to the wilderness, and modern architecture, at least in the hands of Wright, was being directed to that source of inspiration. So, the new need for nature, the almost picture postcard allure of the wild, has been rising as a contemporary desire for decades—gimme shelter, be it in the mountains or the woods, or on a beach, but get me out of the city. This impulse, a very strong one, and perhaps a source of abusive construction in natural settings, has strong roots and surely a good future, at least for those with considerable means.

Living in nature is surely not only in the picture postcard mode—there have always been people who live in forest cabins, tree houses, or beach huts, places that almost by definition are carbon friendly, small, and inexpensive. Thoreau built his cabin from recycled and hand-cut materials for $28.12. It measured just 10 by 15 feet (150 square feet, or 14 square meters), and he described the interior as having a fireplace, table, desk, bed, and three chairs. One must dare to say that this design was the fruit of awareness of the world, and a will to live with and in nature, to seek less rather than more, to be open to the beauty of largely undisturbed nature. Living in nature is not necessarily a contemporary way of being—it depends very much on the degree to which people accept to live with nature. Thoreau's handmade approach and simple means meet both goals—living with and in nature. Modern technology and the awareness of the fragility of the natural environment allow others, more inclined to comfort, to venture out into the wild today, but with the smallest (carbon) footprint possible, and with respect for what is and has been for centuries.

Eight Billion Souls

A world population of nearly eight billion souls does not really leave hope that everyone can live in nature. The homes published here are for the most part reserved to a privileged few, with or without a profound sense of ecological realities. As to living with nature, that is not only the project of an elite, it also must be the broadest of all possible goals—to reduce the pollution and damage that is done to nature to the greatest extent possible. These homes, even the small and very modest ones, are at the rarefied extremity of what is and what can be done in terms of building responsibly. Just as designers like Mike Vensel hope that their efforts and ideas might

opposite Gimme Shelter, Gimme Shelter Solutions

benefit those who have no home at all, so discoveries and techniques may be used in ever broader circles of construction, hopefully bringing down the current monstrous levels of CO_2 and other noxious by-products of "civilization." But the message here need not be so earth-shattering and vast. It is possible too to look at these homes, selected because they are in various ways about living with and in nature, and to imagine dawn on a Norwegian fjord or a bay in Tasmania, to see the sunset on the Pacific coast of Costa Rica or Lake Kawaguchiko. At the same time, as ecological calamity looms large on the horizon, living today offers an unprecedented possibility to see and perhaps to visit the far-flung corners of the earth . . . albeit with an impossibly large carbon footprint. Best to turn the pages and dream.

PHILIP JODIDIO
Lausanne, Switzerland
May 30, 2023

left Aurora Lodge, Snorre Stinessen Architecture

HOUSE AMONG THE PINES

Dnipro, Ukraine, 2022

ARCHOBRAZ, *Dnipro*

COMPLETED IN DNIPRO, very shortly before the Russian offensive against Ukraine began, this house has an area of 2,476 square feet (230 square meters) and was built on a 15,069-square-foot (1,400-square-meter) site. Situated along both sides of the Dnipro River, which effectively divides the country between east and west, the city of nearly a million people has seen country houses built in a radius of about 22 miles (35 kilometers) from the center. The architects carefully developed the design considering the use of natural resources and respect for the forested environment of this house. They engaged in a study not only of the impact of a building on a forest environment, but also questioned the type of architecture best suited to this place and this environment. Passive energy factors were considered for the orientation of the stained-glass windows, which have a built-in winter heating system. A heat pump is used for ventilation, air-conditioning, and heating, as well as hot water. The external cladding is in locally sourced metal and wood. As this book was being prepared, the owners of the house had not returned to live there, but Dnipro was being transformed by immigration from eastern Ukraine, not only of persons, but also of businesses and schools. Although these circumstances could not have been foreseen by the client, nor by the architects, they appear to be taking things in stride given the difficult conditions. Founded by the architect Oleksii Obraztsov in 2002, ArchObraz has worked on numerous public and commercial projects in Ukraine since that time, including large-scale development plans. In April 2023, Obraztsov wrote to the author, "Everything is fine with the house itself. One double-glazed window is damaged, but I do not know the cause of the damage. It is not yet possible to replace such a rare product in the current conditions. Our team still lives and works in Dnipro."

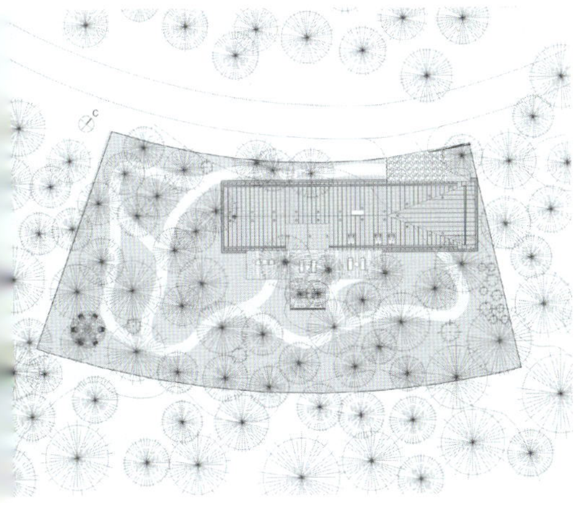

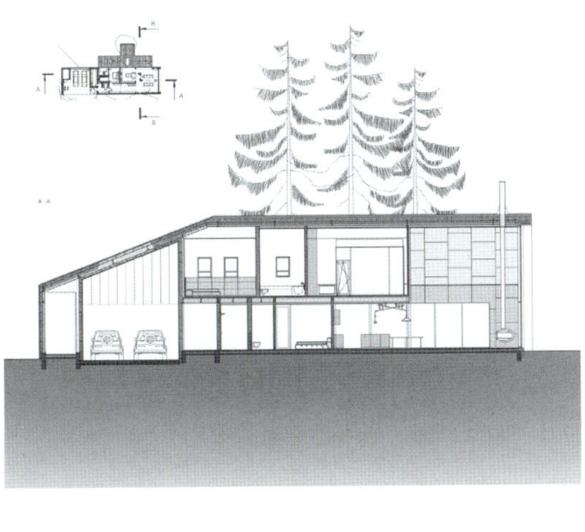

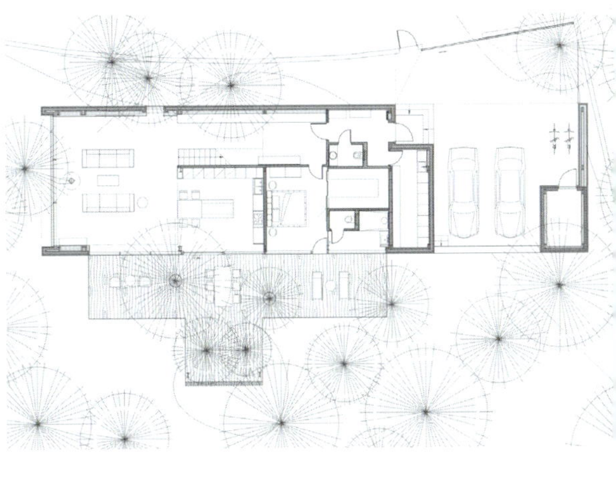

left

The full height glazing of the main facade allows for open views of the forest. A light stairway leads to the upper private areas.

opposite

The impression of openness is confirmed in these two photos, which show different angles of the bedroom.

LA LOMITA

Loma de Rodríguez, Valle de Bravo, Mexico, 2021

ASPJ ARQUITECTURA, *Paisaje y Territorio, Mexico City*

THIS PROJECT WAS CONCEIVED by the landscape architect Hélène Carlo and the industrial designer Emiliano García. Their goal was to create housing that could "be replicable in the basin of Valle de Bravo." The two-level structure includes an office, carpentry workshop, kitchen, living / dining room, two bedrooms, and two bathrooms. The ground floor has an area of 1,023 square feet (95 square meters) while the upper level is smaller (549 square feet / 51 square meters). The house occupies just 20 percent of its 5,382-square-foot (500-square-meter) site. The house was built mostly with recycled plywood used to transport cars and parts for the local automobile industry. The architects explain, "The orientation of the house is designed to take advantage of the climatic conditions in its favor, adapting to the different seasons of the year; it isolates itself from extreme humidity and heat at different times of the year and different hours of the day." An emphasis in the design is put on what is called the *cosecha de agua* (harvesting of water). Rainwater is collected from the roof and reused, with sewage and wastewater treated first by a biodigester and then in wetland space that is part of the garden design. The roof was made with an arch recycled from an unfinished project that is oriented to allow little light penetration during the summer and more in winter. The architects further explain, "The project manages to lower costs due to factors such as the reuse of recycled materials, its lightness, and an efficient work process due to the simplicity of assembly and disassembly. This together makes it easily replicable." Valle de Bravo is a picturesque touristic town located 97 miles (156 kilometers) southwest of Mexico City. Set at an altitude of 6,070 feet (1,850 meters) above sea level and higher, it has a temperate and steady temperature range (40 to 80°F / 4 to 27°C) with vegetation that is dominated by pines. The light structure of this house and its close relation to rain and wet landscaping are, of course, directly influenced by the location.

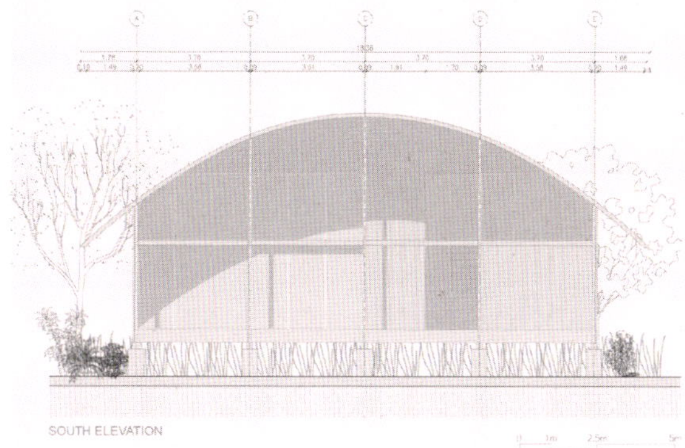
SOUTH ELEVATION

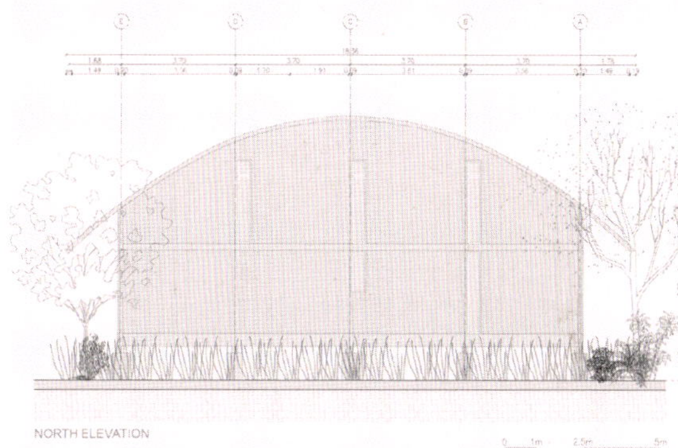
NORTH ELEVATION

previous

The simple arched roof and light wooden structure provide ample exposure to the surrounding landscape.

opposite

A wood-burning stove can give warmth in this region where winter evening temperatures can go below 40°F.

MARRAMARRA SHACK

Marramarra Creek, Berowra, New South Wales, Australia, 2020

LEOPOLD BANCHINI ARCHITECTS,
Geneva, Switzerland

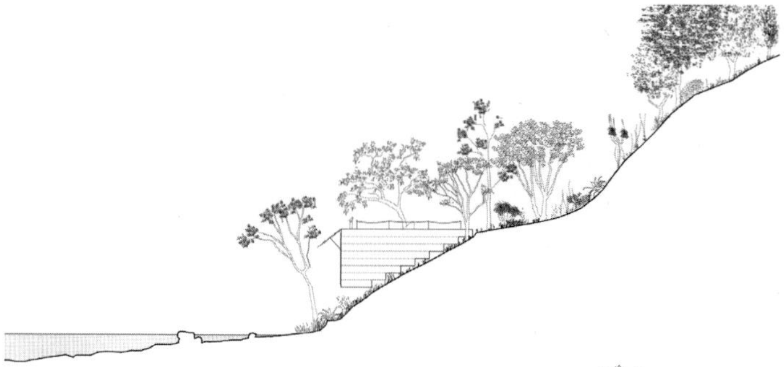

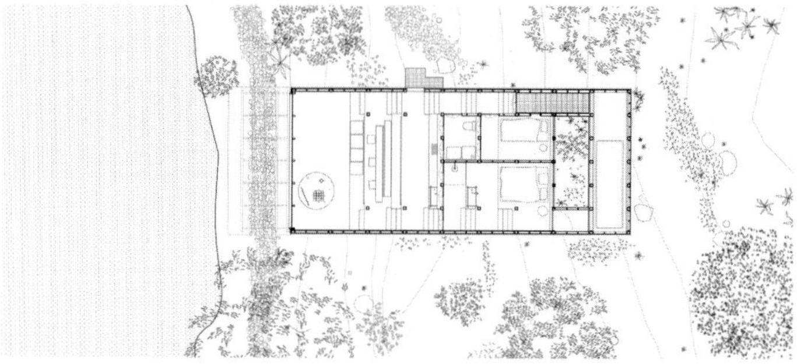

THE MARRAMARRA NATIONAL PARK is a 29,121-acre (11,785-hectare) nature preserve located about 25 miles (40 kilometers) northwest of central Sydney. It encompasses lands of Aboriginal Darug clans. Captain James Cook mapped the nearby area of Broken Bay at the entrance to the Hawkesbury River (originally Dyarubbin) during his exploration of the coast in 1770. The architect Leopold Banchini used reclaimed wood and other local materials to create an ecologically respectful house in this sensitive area. Ironbark (*Eucalyptus crebra*) pillars repurposed from early British electrical posts are combined with local Spotted Gum (*Corymbia maculata*) beams, and details and furnishing made with Turpentine wood (*Syncarpia glomulifera*) recovered from a disused jetty nearby. The pillars sit on sandstone bedrock, obviating the need for added concrete. The site of the house is steeply sloped, and the design steps down the hill assuming a slight cantilever at its lowest point, where a wood-burning stove marks the interior. Tellingly, the Australian structural engineers for this project are called Cantilever Studio. The design emphasizes an operable north-facing window that looks out onto the Marramarra Creek. Two small rooms, a patio, and a roof terrace, form the essential spaces of the Shack. Thin fiber-cement cladding sheets were used to improve the fire resistance of the otherwise wooden dwelling. The entire design was conceived to avoid the use of heavy machinery, and the roof is used to harvest both solar energy and water, assuring an exceptionally low carbon footprint and continued sustainability. The architect Banchini has an unusual profile for this location—he was born in Switzerland in 1981 and studied architecture at the Glasgow School of Art, receiving his diploma from the EPFL (Lausanne). He worked with LOT-EK in New York and b720 Fermín Vázquez Arquitectos in Barcelona before founding his own firms, most recently Leopold Banchini Architects in Geneva. Very much aware of the unusual nature of this Australian site, the architect states, "Marramarra Shack is built on the land of the Darug people. We acknowledge the Traditional Custodians of the land on which the house is set, their rich cultural heritage and deep connection to country, and pay our respects to their Elders past, present, and future. Always was, always will be Aboriginal land."

CABANA

Paraty, Rio de Janeiro, Brazil, 2002/10

BERNARDES ARQUITETURA, *Rio de Janeiro*

BUILT ON A 17.3-ACRE (7-hectare) site that can only be accessed by boat, this is a small forest refuge for the family of one of Rio's best-known architects. Thiago Bernardes was born in Rio de Janeiro in 1974. His grandfather was Sérgio Bernardes, a Brazilian architect who won the Brussels World's Fair prize in 1956. His father was Cláudio Bernardes, founder-partner of Cláudio Bernardes & Jacobsen Arquitetura in Rio. In 1992, he entered Santa Úrsula College in Rio, but preferred to engage in a self-taught career. In 2011, Thiago Bernardes founded Bernardes Arquitetura, with Camila Tariki, Márcia Santoro, Dante Furlan, and Nuno Costa Nunes. They currently have a team of sixty persons with offices in Rio de Janeiro and São Paulo. The design of the 1,292-square-foot (120-square-meter) Cabana follows the disposition of previously existing structures, a boathouse near the water, the cabana, and a higher-level viewing area. The main volume has a wooden deck, kitchen, bathroom, and bedroom. Glulam (glue-laminated timber) was used for the structure together with modular panels made with painted plywood boards, with the whole system designed to be easily transported to the remote site. An electrical generator was placed near a small caretaker's house, and water is available from the site. The architects explain, "The social area is a large balcony, open, connected to nature, sometimes protected by the canopy of trees, sometimes catching sight of the sea between the leaves. At the perimeter, a wooden bench plays the role of guard rails. This space has awnings as the only closure." Paraty, in the state of Rio de Janeiro, is located 160 miles (258 kilometers) southwest from the city of Rio. Its climate corresponds to the informal style of this architecture. The average annual temperature in Paraty is 70.6°F (21.4°C). As Paraty is near the equator (Southern Hemisphere), this temperature is typical year-round, though temperatures range up to 86°F (30°C) in February. Paraty is also characterized by heavy rainfall in January, February, March, November, and December.

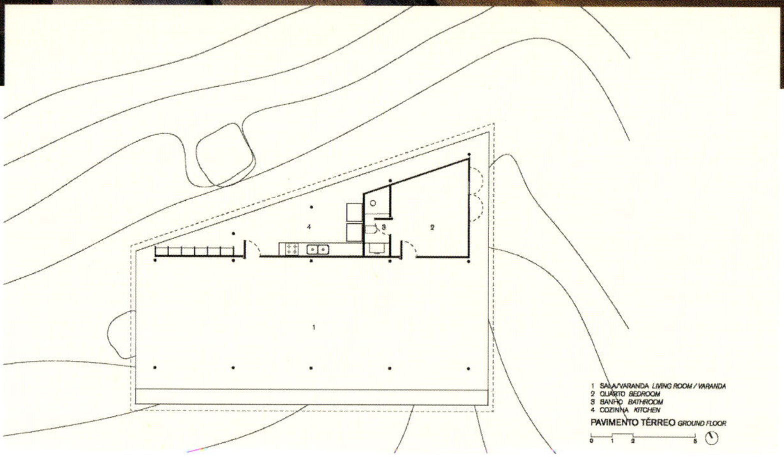

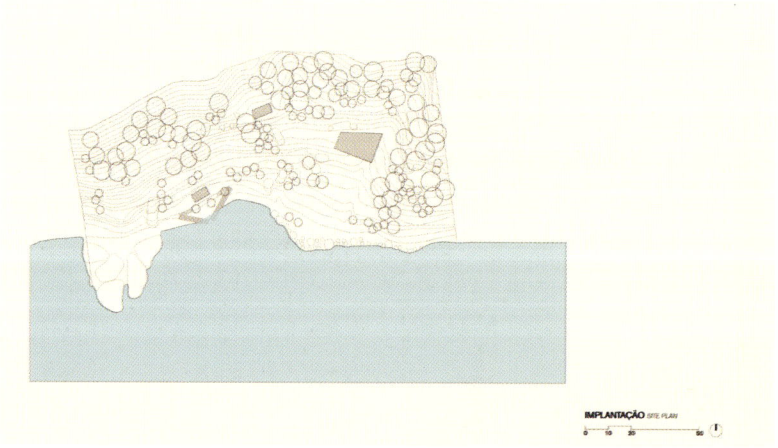

right

Less elaborate than many houses designed by the architects, this is a real modern cabin in the woods, with open interior spaces sheltered only from the rain.

opposite

The house appears to hover above its densely forested site, combining modern lines with an essentially wooden structure.

LOLITA

JUDITE

CAVALCANTE HOUSE

Cavalcante, Goiás, Brazil, 2020

BLOCO ARQUITETOS, *Brazil*

CASA CAVALCANTE IS IN THE CENTER of an area of 657 acres (266 hectares), near the Chapada dos Veadeiros National Park in the vast Brazilian savanna (*Cerrado*). The architects clearly state their intention to minimize the impact of the building on its natural surrounds. In this hot area on a site that is difficult to access and where there is limited qualified labor, their task was not insubstantial. The architects explain, "We defined the construction process in two stages. The first one applied prefabricated elements remotely and assembled at the construction site, while the second used mostly local handmade labor. We . . . decided to construct the semi-industrialized part of the house at first. Its macrostructure is composed of a modular sequence of metallic columns and beams and covered by thermoacoustic roof tiles, also called 'sandwich tiles.' In this way, we were able to provide shade to the workers and protect them from the intense sun while working on the second phase of the work, which used handmade construction processes." The size of available thermoacoustic tiles is directly related to the structural parameters of the house and the pitch of its roof, limiting the need to cut or form parts on-site. Overhanging roofs provide contact between residents and the natural environment. A brise-soleil system made with eucalyptus logs, which doubles as a bug repellent, helps to make the interior environment more comfortable, and natural lighting and ventilation are another feature of the house. The perimeter walls of the 4,306-square-foot (400-square-meter) house were made with local clay (adobe bricks), and the house was raised off the ground to protect the adobe and to keep out creeping animals. Photovoltaic panels provide electricity, and an open area (*aceiro*) was created around the house to protect it from frequent wildfires.

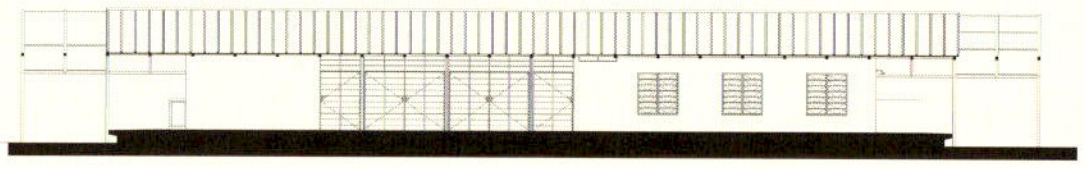

corte AA

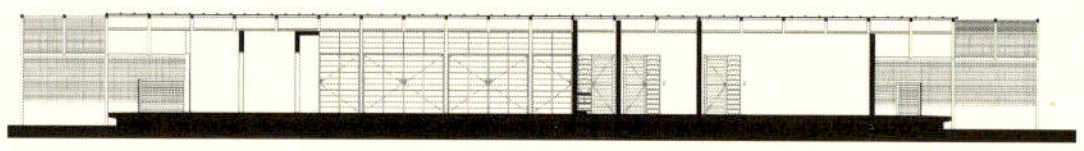

corte BB

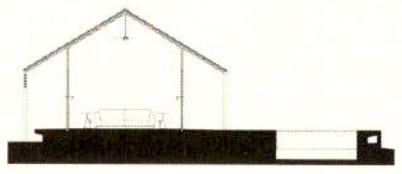

corte CC

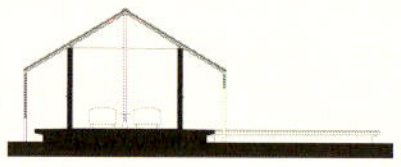

corte DD

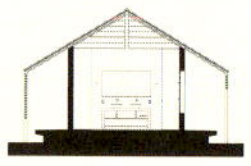

corte EE

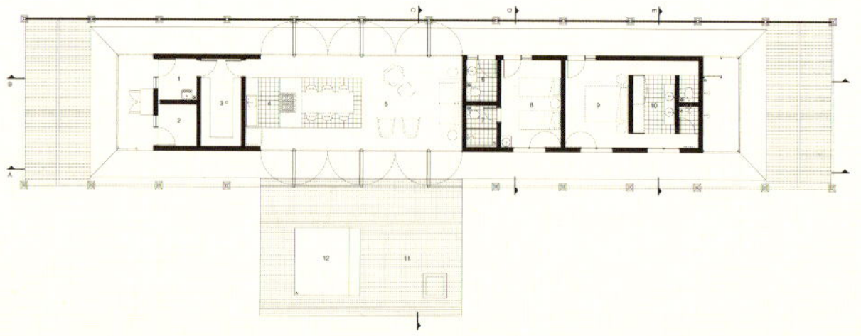

1. Área de Serviço Coberta
2. Depósito
3. Despensa
4. Cozinha
5. Sala de Estar / Jantar
6. Banheiro Social
7. Banheiro Suíte
8. Suíte Hóspedes
9. Suíte Casal
10. Banheiro Casal
11. Deck
12. Piscina

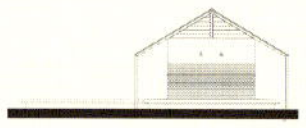

elevação leste

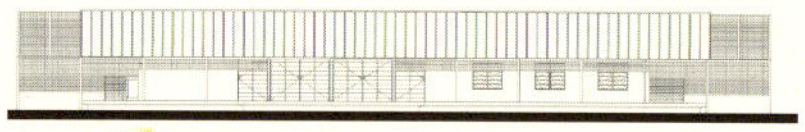

elevação norte

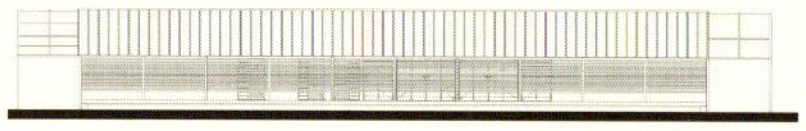

elevação sul

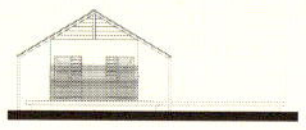

elevação oeste

INSPIRE

left

Very light operable doors allow the interior spaces to be opened entirely to the exterior.

above

Lifted slightly off the ground, the design of the house protects from direct sunlight and encourages cross-ventilation.

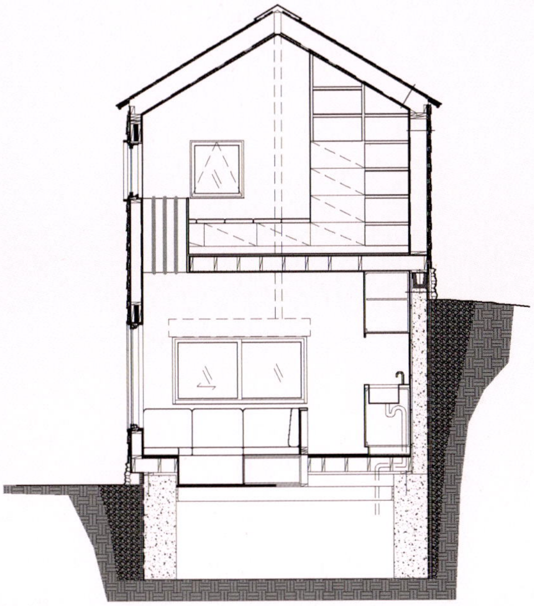

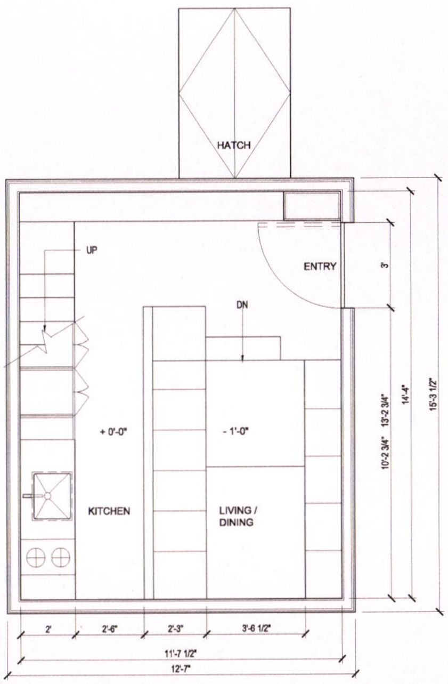

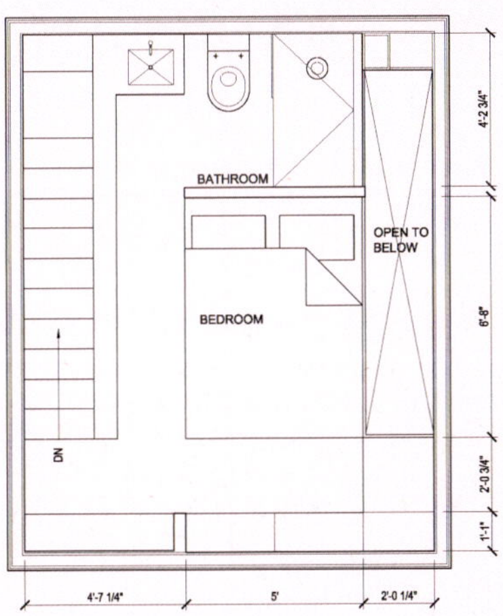

MICRO CABIN

Montauk, New York, United States, 2014

BREITNER CIACCIA—OFFICE OF ARCHITECTURE (BC-OA), *New York*

THIS VERY SMALL STRUCTURE, 323 square feet (30 square meters), was designed as a guest cabin that the architects fixed to an existing foundation with a 12-by-15-foot (3.6-by-4.5-meter) footprint. The architects treated the volume, "smaller than a single car garage, as a little jewel box, packed out with the full functionality of a house four times its size, but efficient and precise to the most minute dimension." The kitchen and storage areas are placed beneath a narrow fir plywood stairway. The kitchen cabinets form the steps, adding to the efficient use of space required for such a small project. The floor in the living area, which is little more than a seating arrangement, is recessed to avoid dividing the room, and a small cast-iron pellet stove has a flue that extends up through the rectangular double-height space to the roof and its skylight. Reclaimed hickory cladding shields the north and west facades of the building from the nearby main house, while openings on the south and east elevations reveal densely grown trees and national forest lands beyond. Although the exterior appearance of the house is rustic, the interiors are comfortably modern. The plan of the structure, which is notched into a slope, is rectangular. Above the kitchen and living area is a bedroom and bathroom, which has a very simple shower in a white-tiled space. Storage space is again tucked beneath the slope of the roof in the bedroom. The Brooklyn-based architects are Bronwyn Breitner, who received her MArch degree from Parsons and worked at Smith-Miller + Hawkinson before co-founding BC-OA, and Luigi Ciaccia, who studied at the New York Institute of Technology and worked previously at the large firms RMJM and KPF.

STEREO
HAWAII

A HOUSE IS NOT A HOME Bruce Weber
SEVEN FIRES

BRILLHUT

North Eleuthera, Bahamas, 2021

BRILLHART ARCHITECTURE, *Miami, Florida*

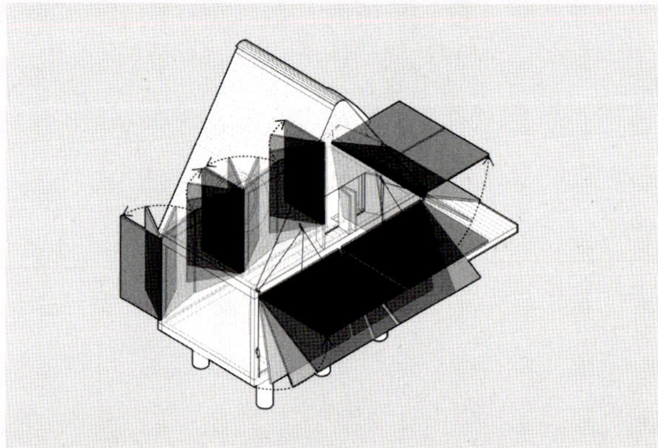

BRILLHART ARCHITECTURE IS A husband-and-wife team based in Miami. They hand-built this small residence with an interior floor area of 700 square feet (65 square meters) plus an 80-square-foot (7.4-square-meter) exterior kitchen with an outdoor shower and bathroom. The Brillhut is inspired in part by local A-frame houses but also by the Maisons Tropicales of the French architect and designer Jean Prouvé and Le Corbusier's Cabanon in the South of France. In 2015, the firm's founder, Jacob Brillhart, published a book of travel drawings executed by Le Corbusier between 1907 and 1911. Like Prouvé, the architects imagined this residence as being a potential prototype for living in a tropical environment. Set up off the ground, the house has a 100-square-foot (9.3-square-meter) exterior terrace. Living and kitchen areas are on the ground floor with the bedroom space under the gabled roof. Skylights in the roof offer residents views of the night sky. The house forms a kind of compound including the main cabin, an outdoor service building, and two storage sheds. It is set 427 feet (130 meters) from the Atlantic Ocean. The cladding is in western red cedar shingles and includes structurally insulated panels (SIPS) that can be closed to protect the residence in the event of (frequent) hurricanes. Solar power and rainwater collection help to make the off-grid house livable. The architects test-assembled the structure in Miami before taking it apart and sending it to Eleuthera. It was intended "to be affordable; easy to build; and designed to be shipped from Florida in a 40-yard (2,391-cubic-foot, 67.7-cubic-meter) container."

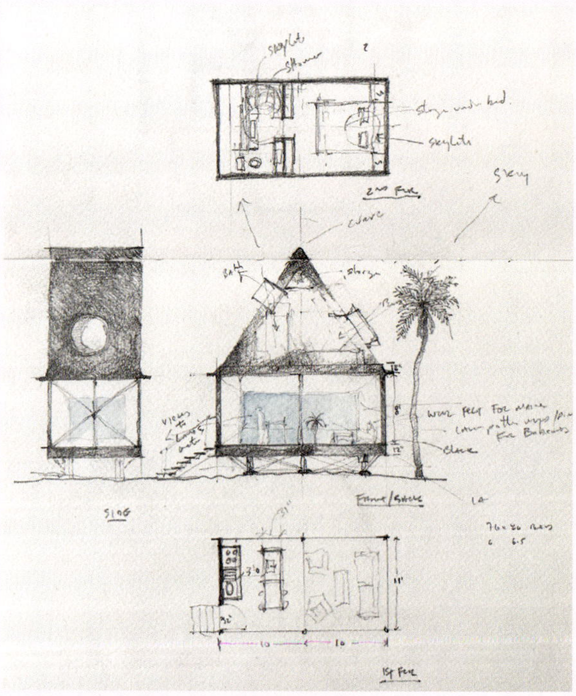

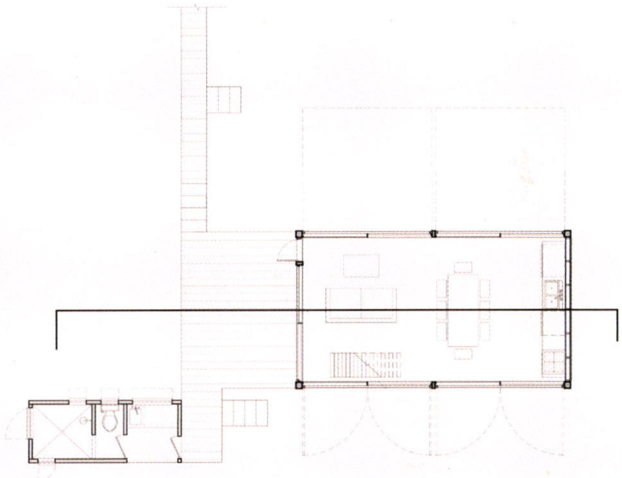

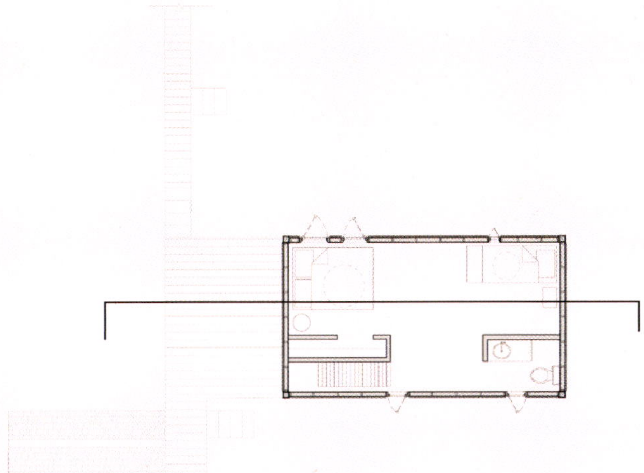

above

A very simple design, as seen in the plans above for this wooden house, does recall the Prouvé houses that inspired its forms.

CRACKENBACK FARM HOUSE

Crackenback, New South Wales, Australia, 2018

CASEY BROWN ARCHITECTURE, *Sydney*

BUILT IN THE SNOWY MOUNTAINS of southern New South Wales, the Crackenback Farm House is part of a group of buildings including this main house, stables, managers quarters, and a machinery shed, all designed by Casey Brown. The architecture references "the Australian vernacular tradition of metal clad rural buildings." Sheltered from the other buildings by the hilly terrain, the house features a 9.8-foot-high (3-meter) forward-sloping panoramic window in the living/dining/kitchen area. The interior features a sculptural concrete stair lit from above with colored skylights. Despite the rural location, the house has every sign of a comfortable, modern residence. The sophisticated metallic appearance of the exterior makes the transition from rurality to twenty-first-century living seem natural. The rectangular building has a north-south alignment and is wrapped in Zincalume and has Corten (weathered steel) extremities. In this environment, at altitude, the building is naturally designed to alternatively resist snowstorms and brush fires. Heat is provided by a wood-burning hydronic (warm water) system and electricity through solar panels. Although being "off-grid" is now seen as a contribution to environmental sustainability, it should be recalled that this type of rural building was almost never connected to municipal electricity and water. Technology in energy and construction systems permits the Crackenback Farm to be both off-grid and comfortable, and that is the main lesson to be noted here in ecological terms. The 4,305-square-foot (400-square-meter) residence was built mainly with corrugated iron, Corten steel, and timber. The architect, Robert Brown, studied at the University of New South Wales and did graduate work at Columbia University (New York, 1992–93). He created Casey Brown in 2004 with Caroline Casey.

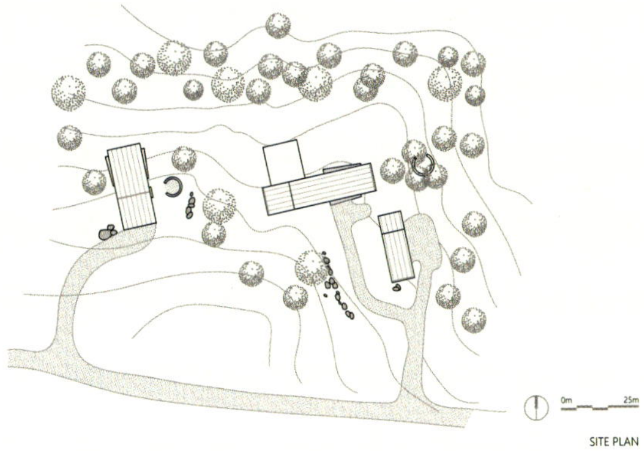

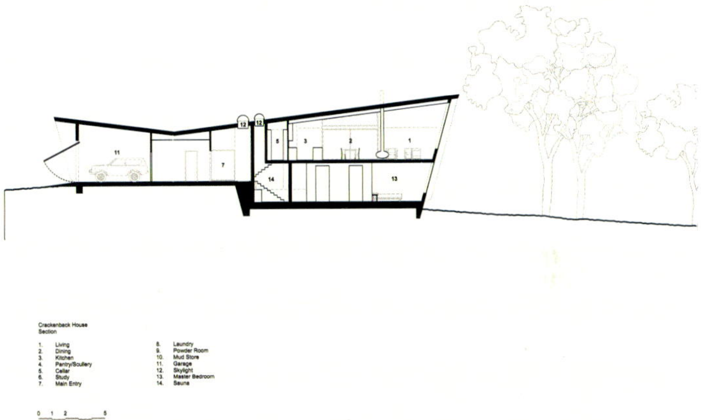

opposite

The sloped roof gives space that rises toward the glazed openings of the living room.

left

Wooden surfaces and circular skylights give a warm natural feeling to the interiors.

above

A site plan and a section drawing of the house show the house from the same angle as the photo above.

HOUSE IN THE FOREST

Rankoshi, Hokkaido, Japan, 2020

FLORIAN BUSCH ARCHITECTS, *Tokyo*

SET NEAR THE DEVELOPING ski resort area of Niseko in southwestern Hokkaido, this house was built on a forested 7.4-square-acre (3-square-hectare) site. The architects explain, "Enchanted by the beauty of the region but disturbed by relentlessly encroaching pseudo-suburbia, the owners, a large family, sought escape in the solitude of the forest. Consequentially, the brief was not for a house but for a time in and with the forest." The house was built at the edge of an existing clearing in the pine forest. From above, the complex design resembles a branch placed between the trees, which are seen through large windows both as a "distant background and a tactile environment." The result of the design and the windows is that "we are sitting in the forest," according to the architects. Each branch of the plan is "cut off" to allow open views that can be perceived along the central spine of the residence. The timber frame of the 2,476-square-foot (230-square-meter) structure was built on a raised reinforced concrete slab. According to Florian Busch, "The House in the Forest is not about a fixed form but an ever-changing dialogue with the forest. The house that was eventually built is merely the result in a process of probing and responding to the surroundings to create a place where the family can be both together and by themselves, where they can become part of the forest." The exterior cladding is in vertical wood strips—the interiors are typically minimal in their appearance, with the full-height bay windows at the end of each branch ramification providing the most essential aspect of the rapport between the architecture and the forest. Florian Busch Architects (FBA) is based in Tokyo. The firm's founder-owner studied architecture in Germany, Japan, and the UK. After graduating from Bauhaus University, Weimar, and the Architectural Association in London, he worked for Toyo Ito & Associates in Tokyo (2004–2008) before creating FBA in 2009.

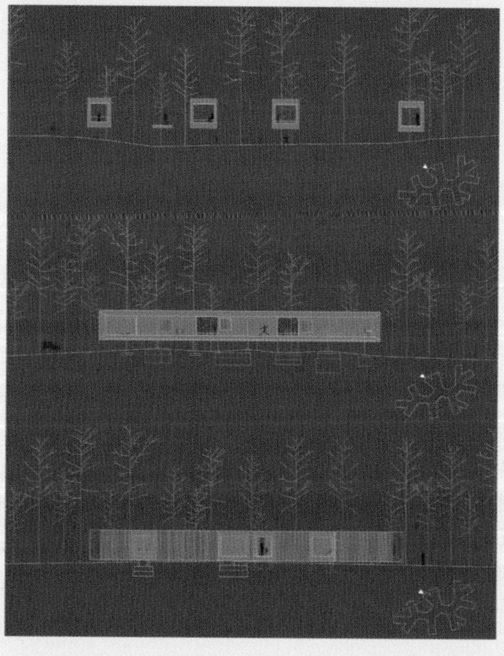

previous

The elegant design exudes a kind of simplicity that characterizes Japanese architecture.

opposite

Lifted off the ground on thin pilotis, the house makes ample use of wood, allowing it to blend into the forested environment.

CASA GIRASOL / SUNFLOWER HOUSE

Valle de Bravo, Mexico, 2023

DEREK DELLEKAMP,
JACHEN SCHLEICH, *Mexico City*

THE CLIENT FOR THIS HOUSE sought "a retreat in the woods but with the security and facilities of a country club." He found a half-acre (2,275-square-meter) lot on a steep wooded site in Rancho Avándaro, near the Valle de Bravo. The circular design of the Sunflower House was chosen to avoid facades directly facing two neighboring houses, to offer views of the trees, and to admit sunlight at any hour of the day. The height of the continuous band window was calculated to admit only views of treetops and the sky, with a skylight admitting further natural illumination. The house was built with pigmented in-situ concrete with wooden formwork, on a base made of local stone. Both the rough concrete and its color were chosen to integrate the house with the forest of pines and oaks. The thermal mass of the concrete walls, of course, provides warmth during cool evenings, reducing the need for any heating to just a few days a year. The roof, interior panels, and ceilings were made with oak. Solar panels and a compact sewage treatment plant, which produces water for the garden, were part of the sustainability scheme of the design. The house has a generous floor area of 6,296 square feet (585 square meters). The architects state, "The functional furniture with few supporting objects and art pieces sits freely in the space and lets the experience of the play of light and shadow on the surfaces in combination with the gentle flow of air and the presence of the vegetation create a constantly changing experience throughout the day." Full-height, glazed doors open entirely to the almost entirely enclosed rear patio of the house. The house was designed by the Mexico City firms Dellekamp Arquitectos and Jachen Schleich | Locus.

left Set in a wooded slope, the house almost disappears amongst the trees.

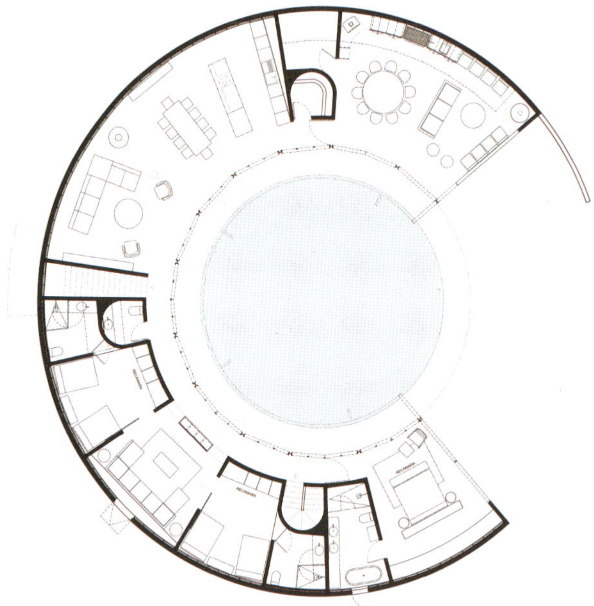

left

The ample kitchen, dining, and living space faces fully opening glazed doors on the side of the inner courtyard.

above

A plan and a section drawing of the house.

HOUSE OVER THE SEA

Surry, Maine, United States, 2014

ELLIOTT ARCHITECTS, *Blue Hill, Maine*

THIS RESIDENCE WAS LITERALLY built above the shore in southeastern Maine. It is located not far from Mount Desert Island, known as a summer haven of parts of the American establishment, and 22 miles (35 kilometers) from Acadia National Park. The House over the Sea has an area of 1,478 square feet (137 square meters). It was built on a steep site measuring 5,570 square feet (517 square meters). The exterior of the building is finished in oiled eastern white cedar shingles. The decking is in ipe wood (*Handroanthus*). Inside, clear maple flooring is used, together with limestone tile in the entrance and guest bathroom. Because the shoreline is subject to erosion, the house is built on a series of piers set on a ledge beneath the beach. Seawalls and other stabilization are also part of the project. The volume and location of the house were based on a pre-existing structure on the site. Most of the allowed volume was oriented to the water, and the single-slope roof also slants in that direction. Passive ventilation was created using high clerestory windows together with large doors and windows. Corey Papadopoli, the project architect, explains, "It was a critical project requirement that the home engage the water both visually and physically. From inside, unobstructed views are achieved through floor to ceiling glass, allowing the expanse of the bay to act as backdrop to the activity inside. At high tide the water comes under the house providing a sense that one is floating above the sea, lending a feeling of tranquility to the space above. A set of stone steps from the terrace below descends to the beach and into the water at high tide, providing immediate immersion into the sea."

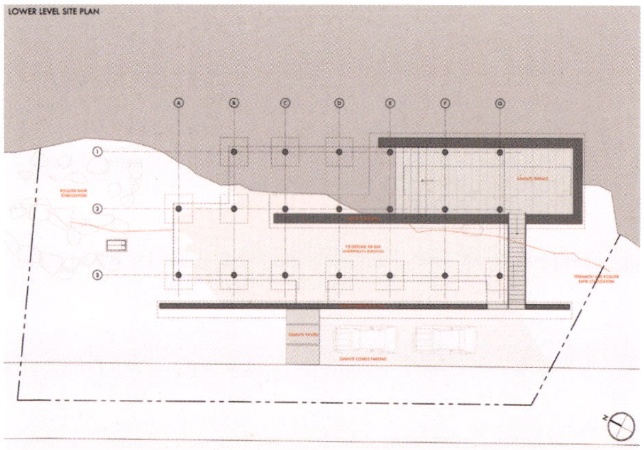

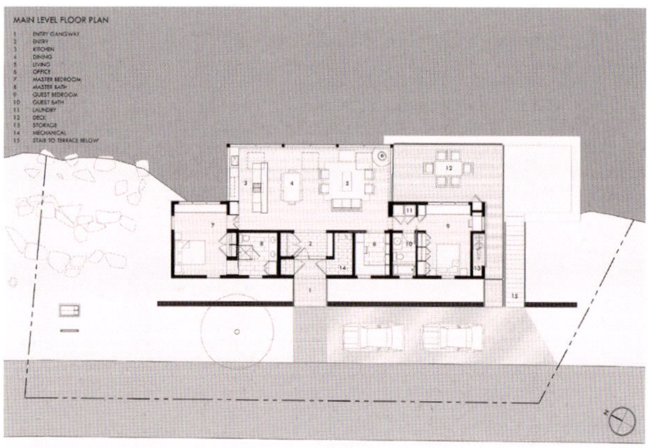

above

A perspective and two plan drawings of the house.

right

Despite its very open design, the house at its entrance does convey a sense of privacy, always emphasized by light.

opposite

On the water side, the residence opens broadly, providing views and bringing in ample natural light. A wood-burning stove heats the living area.

ACHIOTÉ

Playa Hermosa en Osa, Costa Rica, 2022

FORMAFATAL, *Prague, the Czech Republic*

DESIGNED BY THE CZECH ARCHITECT Dagmar Štěpánová, these two "minimalist" villas intended for short-term rental were built with rammed earth on a steep site overlooking the Pacific. Clay from the excavation was used directly to build the perimeter load-bearing walls. The architect states, "Both villas were designed with respect to sustainability and the surrounding wild environment." Set on a 2.7-square-acre (11,000-square-meter) site, the architecturally identical houses each have a floor area of 969 square feet (90 square meters). The architect explains, "My intention was to design sustainable houses with biophilic interiors, which will be sophisticatedly thought-up and at the same time their shaping will be strongly minimalist and simple. No unnecessary extra element, but also nothing to miss. The architecture of villas with its thin and sharp lines is deliberately in contrast to lush tropical vegetation, but the chosen materials and colors coincide perfectly with the surroundings." Because of the dense vegetation, the location of the houses, just 39 feet (12 meters) apart, allows for complete privacy. The houses are differentiated in terms of their internal décor. The first, called Jaspis, is "connected to the ocean and the sky" through its sand-shaded coloring. The architect compares this scheme to a "yin" energy as opposed to the "yang" of the other house, the Nefrit Villa, with its red/terra-cotta-colored concrete floor. Infinity pools emphasize the feeling of a direct connection with the waters of the Pacific, visible beyond. Aside from the rammed earth walls, the houses have structural steel H-beams, supporting monolithic concrete slab ceilings. Štěpánová states, "I chose materials that are as durable as possible considering the Costa Rican climate and high humidity. To realize the clay rammed earth walls, I invited an experienced specialist from Brazil, the owner of Terra Compacta company, because in Costa Rica no one had experience with this construction method. Daniel Mantovani from Terra Compacta trained several local craftsmen, and together they can claim credit for having completed the first rammed earth buildings in Costa Rica." The houses have frameless windows and no doors except for a sliding panel that provides privacy for the shower and toilet.

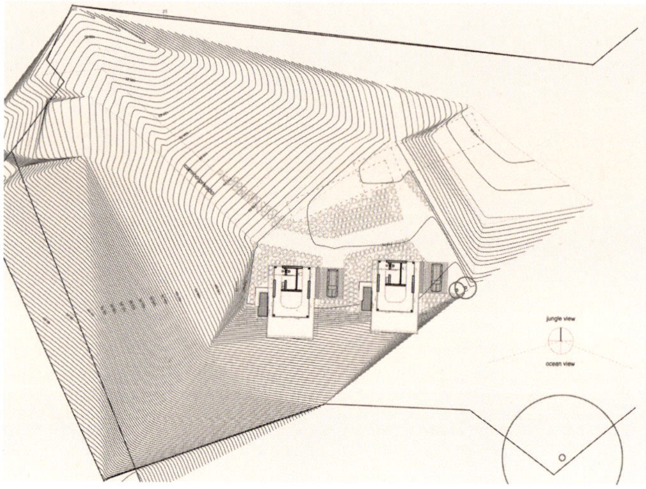

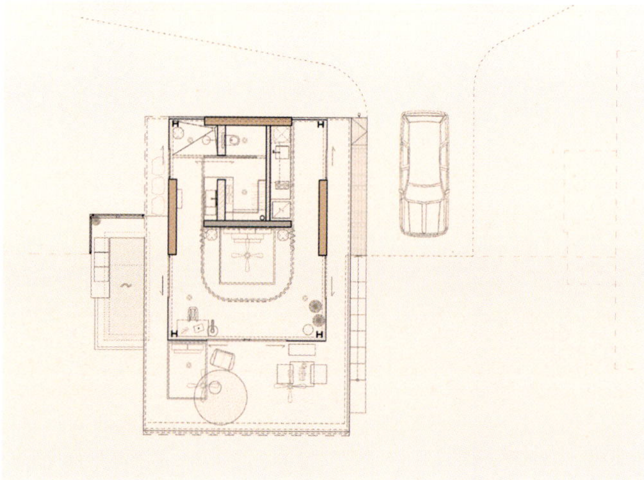

above

A site plan, floor plan, and section drawing of the house at the edge of a steep slope.

following

The house almost appears to be floating in the jungle, an effect that can be understood from the section drawing above.

GIMME SHELTER

Väddö, Sweden, 2021

GIMME SHELTER SOLUTIONS, *Stockholm*

VÄDDÖ IS AN 18.6-MILE-LONG (30-kilometer) island in the Baltic Sea located about an hour and a half from Stockholm. With a floor area of just 430 square feet (42 square meters) this cabin is located on a 2,500-square-meter (26,910-square-foot) forested site. The larger of the two volumes contains a living room, kitchen, and bathroom—a smaller (108 square foot, 10 square meter) one is for the bedroom. It was designed and built by Emelie Holmberg, who is the founder of Gimme Shelter. Her concept consists of making houses with "several pieces/modules, like LEGO, that can be put together in various alterations. The modules are predesigned so they can be manufactured industrially, but the system makes the design of the houses flexible because of the many ways the modules can be put together. The industrial part makes the houses more cost-efficient, and the flexibility makes the building still unique. The LEGO system makes it possible to start with one module, and with time, budget, and if the family grows, it can be extended organically with new modules. The sustainability lies in the natural materials the house consists of—almost only wood—but also the way to live without unnecessary space for building, heat, and maintenance." In a gesture that recalls some elements of Japanese architecture, the house has a veranda with an overhanging roof that protects the outdoor space, linking it more closely to the interiors but also to the natural setting. Sliding wooden panels can close off the verandas, recalling the sliding panels of Japan but also elements of Swedish agricultural buildings. The deck projects partially into the woods at right angles to the houses, which "reinforces the sense of being immersed in nature." Holmberg explained, "The architectural work is all my own. I did all the drawings for it and 3D models. I financed the project and was part of the team that built it, which made it possible for me to control the whole building process. A lot was designed on-site as we were building the house. You often don't discover whether drawings work until they become 3D elements, built to scale. In this project, if something didn't look the way I had originally visualized it, I could change it until I was happy with the result" (Archdaily). This project is intriguing because it combines a natural, ecologically sustainable approach in the context of a design and construction method that can be considered industrial, or at any rate modular, as Holmberg says. She has invested her own money and time in an effort to find a new way to build and live in a natural setting.

HOUSE IN THE HILLS

Barrabool, Victoria, Australia, 2018

SEAN GODSELL ARCHITECTS, *Fitzroy, Victoria*

BUILT IN AN AREA OF Australia subject to cold southerly winds, the design of the house is in good part influenced by this fact. The living area and courtyard face north and are protected from the wind by the "re-shaped landscape" but also by a 98-by-98-foot (30-by-30-meter) louvered parasol. Although he clearly references the steel-framed hay sheds that are typical of the Australian countryside, the architect, Sean Godsell, also refers to the Pavilion Le Corbusier in Zürich, Switzerland (1967), which makes use of a protective "free-floating" roof. Of course, in an Australian rural setting, the idea of shelter is defined differently than in Zürich. Godsell says, "Notions of the frontier, of survival in a never-ending battle with nature, are close to the bone for many Australians. In the Outback, any constructed shelter can mean the difference between life and death—shade from the intense heat, height above the flooding river so that these simple, often weather-ravaged structures assume a more profound meaning." Built on a 64-acre (25.9-hectare) site, the house has a total floor area of 1,668 square feet (155 square meters) but a much larger roof area of 9,687 square feet (900 square meters) because of the louvered parasol. Aside from the large square parasol, the house forms an L shape, with the living room forming the juncture between the public spaces and three bedrooms. Much like the parasol itself, the house assumes a hard, efficient appearance both inside and out. Built with a braced steel frame, the house is made mostly with steel and timber. Barrabool is a rural town with a population of about 250 people. It is 47 miles (76 kilometers) southwest of Melbourne. Godsell was born in Melbourne in 1960. He graduated from the University of Melbourne in 1984 and worked from 1986 to 1988 in London with Denys Lasdun. He created his own firm in 1994 and was the winner of the 2022 Australian Institute of Architects Gold Medal. The jury citation read in part, "Godsell's work has contributed significantly by expressing, on a global stage, an architectural response to Australia's unique landscape."

above and right

Godsell's very simple crisp lines create a generous, open interior space.

following

Full-height sliding windows give the impression that the interior of the house has joined itself into the wide landscape.

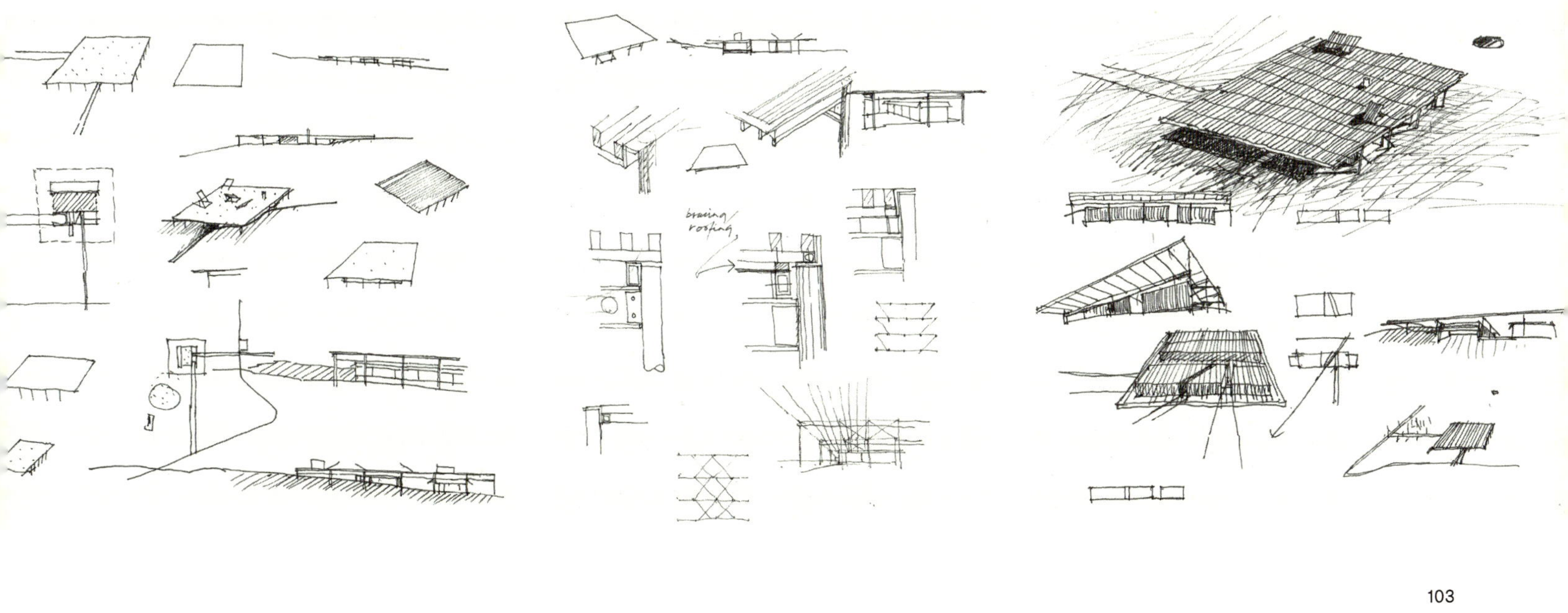
bracing
roofing

CASA DETIF

Chiloé Island, Chile, 2021

GUILLERMO ACUÑA ARQUITECTOS ASOCIADOS (GAAA), *Santiago*

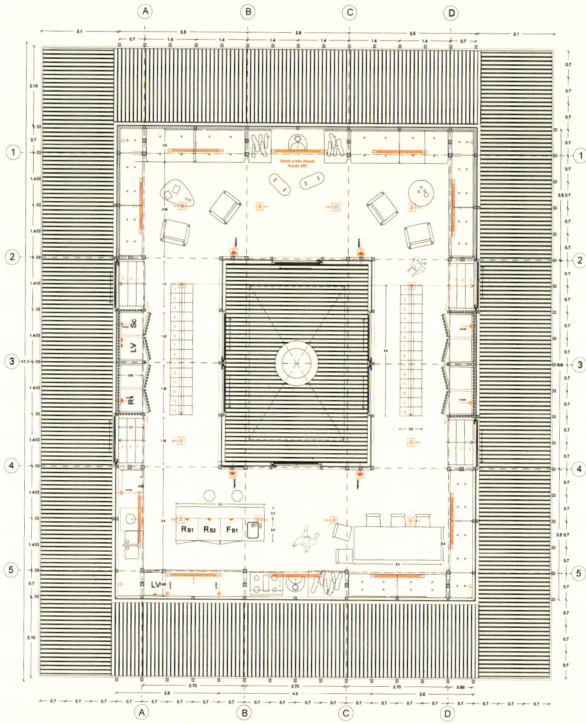

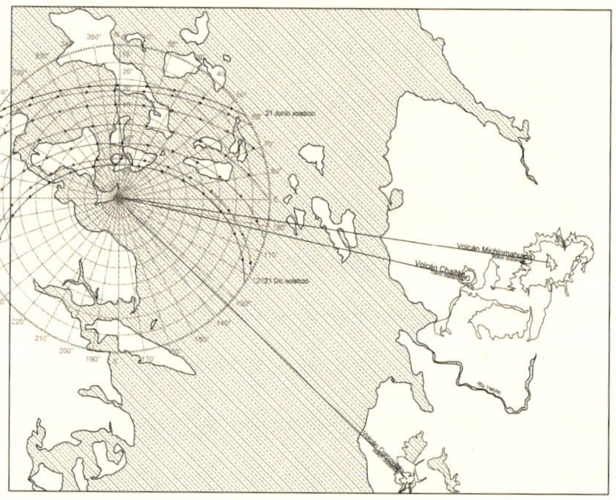

DETIF IS LOCATED ON THE INNER shore of Chiloé Island, about 621 miles (1,000 kilometers) south of Santiago. The 2,099-square-foot (195-square-meter) Detif house is built on stilts on a steep slope that offers views of the water. The architect Guillermo Acuña was born in Santiago, Chile. He studied architecture at the Pontificia Universidad Católica de Chile (Santiago, 1985–91), and created his own firm, GAAA, in 1991. He explains that he places a focus on traditional and vegetal materials "to express the possibilities of the orders of the vegetal kingdom and traditional construction in wood and fibers, which can go on to manifest the impressive geography of Chile." In this instance, he was inspired by local vernacular architecture that relies on stilts to obviate the risks of flooding and coastal erosion. Traditional designs allow houses to be moved to other locations when circumstances warrant. The house is organized around a central courtyard and surrounded by decks that are supported by the stilts. The lowest level includes a living room and kitchen, with bedrooms and bathrooms on the next flight up. The foundation and ground floor of the house are placed amongst the tree trunks, with the upper floor sitting in the foliage. The site offered restricted access, which meant that the house had to be built with relatively small elements. Modular CNC milled panels were made with locally sourced pine. Carried to the site, the pieces were then assembled by three carpenters according to a manual produced by the architects. GAAA participates in an initiative called Fundación Reforestemos. For this project, they calculated the number of trees used for construction and replanted an equal number of native trees. The architect Guillermo Acuña uses an interesting mixture of local knowledge and unexpected imagery to explain his work. He writes, "In 1822 John Ayrton invented the Thaumatrope, built to demonstrate the persistence of the image on the retina. A small disk with two images, an empty cage and a bird, when rotating by stretching two simple strings, made us perceive the first cinematographic movement when the two images are superimposed on the retina. It is not by chance that Ayrton chose these two images to inaugurate a new form of perception. Our perception of the world would no longer be how we experience it, but how we see it. Science would convince us that true reality is a more or less abstract world behind the world we perceive, a world devoid of qualities, temperature, warmth, color, smell, taste, hardness or softness, senses through which we relate to Nature prior to knowledge. In such a way that what one perceives can be misleading, and how to be sure that what remains caged or locked up, is inside or outside?" Acuña clearly pleads with this house for a different kind of sustainable architecture that returns not only to nature but to unaltered perception of space, light, and time.

previous

Set up on a wooden platform on a sloped site, the house has a surprising transparency highlighted by its red structure.

left

The red color of the wood is carried through to this interior courtyard volume.

following

The light structure opens almost entirely to the forested environment.

CASA QUILANTO

Fundo Leona, Los Ríos, Chile, 2022

HEBRA ARQUITECTOS, *Vitacura, Chile*

AN OBJECTIVE OF THIS DESIGN was to disturb the forest site as little as possible—thus the house was built on *pilotis*, or piles, obviating the need for excavation and allowing existing trees to grow through the deck. The site area is 2 hectares (just under 5 acres), and the house itself has a floor area of 1,184 square feet (110 square meters) with a further 646 square feet (60 square meters) of outdoor deck space on either side of the public space. The kitchen, dining area, and living room are near the center of the structure, where the highest space is located. Sliding glass doors allow residents to move freely through the central living space from one deck to another. The middle volume is in fact fully glazed from floor to ceiling, creating not only a smooth transition between interior and exterior but also a feeling of being entirely surrounded by and within the forest. Bedrooms are at either extremity of the rectangular plan, with the main bedroom on one side and two smaller ones at the opposite side, with a sliding partition designed to create a guest space. The architects explain, "Due to a limited budget, the house was very simple in terms of finishing. The exterior façade was covered in cypress in a natural tone, while the same wooden plywood used as a part of the wall structure was kept on the interior walls and ceiling. With the same logic of keeping costs down, the floor was defined as polished concrete." It might well be the budgetary constraints and the effort to fully integrate this house into its forest setting that give the Casa Quilanto such a contemporary appeal—it seems to hover above its forest setting, ready to move on when the time comes without devastating the forest floor. In the meantime, it allows its residents to be fully immersed in the natural environment. Fundo Leona is north of Lago Ranco, a twelve-hour bus ride south from Santiago—574 miles (924 kilometers) away by road.

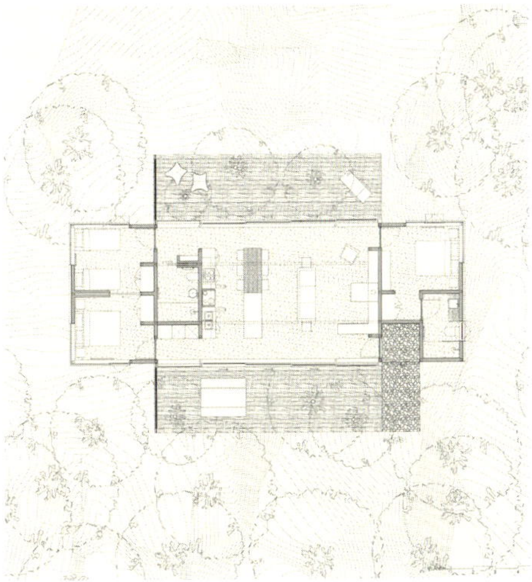

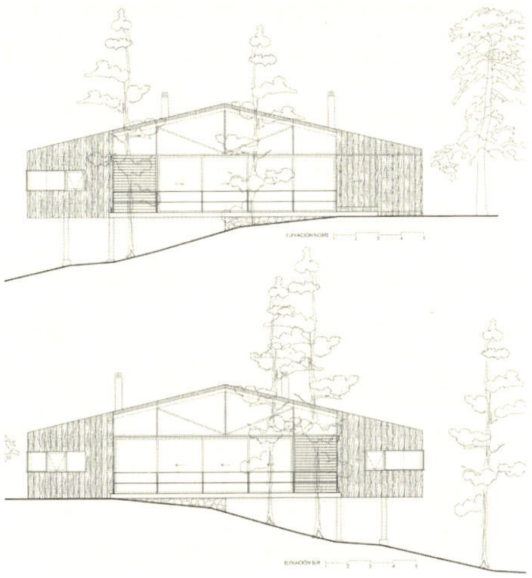

LANDABURU BORDA

Bera, Navarre, Spain, 2019

JORDI HIDALGO TANÉ, *Barcelona*

BERA IS A TOWN in northeastern Spain, in the Basque region near the French border. The Landaburu Borda is a small traditional building located a few kilometers from Bera in a wooded rural setting. The architect says, "To work in this exceptional location is an exercise of respect to the fragile building and especially to the mystical power of the Navarre mountains, rich in history and legends." In an unusual architectural choice, Hidalgo Tané added a subterranean volume connected to the old house by a glass corridor. This decision allowed the architect to hide the extension almost completely in the hillside near the older house. He says, "The program consists in a rural house with a few rooms in the existing building, and a spacious annex with a living area with kitchen built inside the mountain, becoming part of it, as if the annex had been there before the old structure was built.... Sheltered inside this 'cave,' we can observe the magnificent landscape." The concrete annex is tucked into the hillside and has a green roof but an entirely glazed front façade. A thin line of skylights at the back of the annex brings natural light into the space and gives the impression that the concrete slab roof is almost floating over the new space. The kitchen and storage areas are located at the back of the annex. The kitchen is fitted out with a concrete counter and wood cabinetry. The residence has a floor area of 4,628 square feet (430 square meters). This very interesting project combines old and new in a convincing way, and at the same time it takes into account the heritage and spirit of an old European area. The green roof and the insertion into the site make the modern addition respectful of the landscape and also improve its environmental sustainability.

POBBLE HOUSE

Dungeness, Kent, UK, 2014

HOLLAWAY STUDIO, *London*

THIS PROJECT IS IN THE Dungeness Estate, a private property on a promontory of the South Coast of Kent, which is part of a National Nature Reserve but also has the Dungeness nuclear power stations nearby. The site of the house measures 31,872 square feet (2,961 square meters), and the house itself 1,130 square feet (105 square meters). *Pobble* is an old Kentish word for pebble. Due to local building regulations, the new house is based on the scale and proportion of an earlier dwelling on the site. The main section, with the kitchen, dining, and living spaces with large-scale glazing opening to the landscape, is clad in larch. The corner of the living area has a corner glazed sliding door that allows the space to open fully to the exterior. Bedrooms and bathrooms are oriented to maximize views and are connected along a corridor that runs the full length of the residence. Another area connected by a glazed corridor includes a children's bedroom, while a third volume is reserved to the entrance, connecting to the dining area. Set up on concrete pillars to minimize impact on the existing natural surface, the house is covered with the larch already mentioned, Corten steel, and cement fiberboard. The architects state, "Pobble House forms a beautifully crafted home which seeks to continue Dungeness's curious architectural legacy and has delivered an exceptionally high-quality family home for our client and their growing family." The point of Dungeness projects approximately 3 miles (4.8 kilometers) into the English Channel. Its austere flat appearance is not contradictory with its rich natural environment, which includes a bird sanctuary and an area protected from any future development. The overall site was bought by EDF Energy in 2017. The Pobble House stands out a bit from its environment because of the color of its larch cladding in these photos, but it has since turned silver-gray. This modern house sits lightly on its curious natural environment—which is apparently due to be engulfed by rising sea levels within 150 years.

above and right

The relatively simple volumes sit lightly on their site, almost as if they could be lifted and carried away.

following

Although the idea is that this house should recall the scale and proportions of a structure previously on the site, it has a decidedly contemporary appearance.

HOUSE IN COIQUE

Lago Ranco, Los Ríos, Chile, 2021

CRISTIÁN IZQUIERDO LEHMANN, *Santiago*

THE PILLARS AND BEAMS of this guest pavilion for a vacation home on Lake Ranco were made with glulam plywood. The balloon-frame walls were filled with projected pulp insulation. Exterior cladding is in heat-treated wood, and plywood was used for the interiors. The basic floors are in concrete, with eucalyptus used for the bedroom floors. The lower floor has a circular plan offering 360-degree views. It is made up of eighteen identical pillar and beam modules with three interior pillars and beams. This ground level includes the living, kitchen, and dining spaces. On the upper floor, three bedrooms are placed in "autonomous boxes" that project from the circular base and open to the natural setting and are arranged in a triangular form around the glazed, circular base. An off-center spiral staircase echoes the slight, intentional "mismatching" of alignments that gives more movement and freedom to the design than might otherwise have been the case. The architect states, "The univocal order of the circle and the multiple order of the triangle have as many fractures as points of contact." Built on a 4.94-acre (2-hectare) site, the pavilion has a floor area of 1,474 square feet (137 square meters). Set up from the ground on a concrete platform, the house suggests a kind of treehouse, where residents seem to float in the lower branches of the forested site. Cristián Izquierdo Lehmann received his degrees in architecture from the Pontificia Universidad Católica de Chile in 2009 (Santiago) and Columbia University (New York, 2014). He is the son of the founders of his firm, Izquierdo Lehmann, Luis Izquierdo, and Antonia Lehmann.

above

Set up off the ground, the residence gives a light, airy feeling, which is confirmed by its interiors.

right

Here, a spiral staircase rises to the upper level—the living space is almost entirely glazed and heated by a wood-burning stove.

HALF-TREE HOUSE

Sullivan County, New York, United States, 2016

JACOBSCHANG, *New York*

THE SMALL 360-SQUARE-FOOT (33-square-meter) house was built on a remote 60-acre (24-hectare) site. The house is entirely off-grid, it has neither running water nor electricity. Adding to the difficulties of the design, the structure had a limited budget, and was built on a slope with no vehicular access. Amateur "weekend builders" had little more than shovels to prepare the terrain. Lifted off the ground, as its name implies, half of the weight of the house is carried by two neighboring trees, while the upper section is anchored with Sonotube footings, which are cardboard tubes filled with concrete to form cylindrical pillars. This configuration means that the house hangs over the forest floor on its lower side. Eastern pines from the property were used to mill the exterior and interior boards. Exterior surfaces were treated with Scandinavian pine tar to improve resistance to weather-related aging. Heating is provided by a Jøtul (Norwegian cast iron) woodstove, although a portable generator has also been brought to the house. The architects further explain that "engineered wood beams form the perimeter with standard nominal lumber for all intermediate framing. Three 2.4-by-2.4-meter (8-by-8-foot) steel-tube pivot doors, the largest single expense, were fabricated offsite and installed, weather-stripped, and fitted onsite with dual-insulated glass." The plan of the house forms an irregular pentagon with storage space to the back, and a bed, kitchenette, and dining area occupying the basic interior.

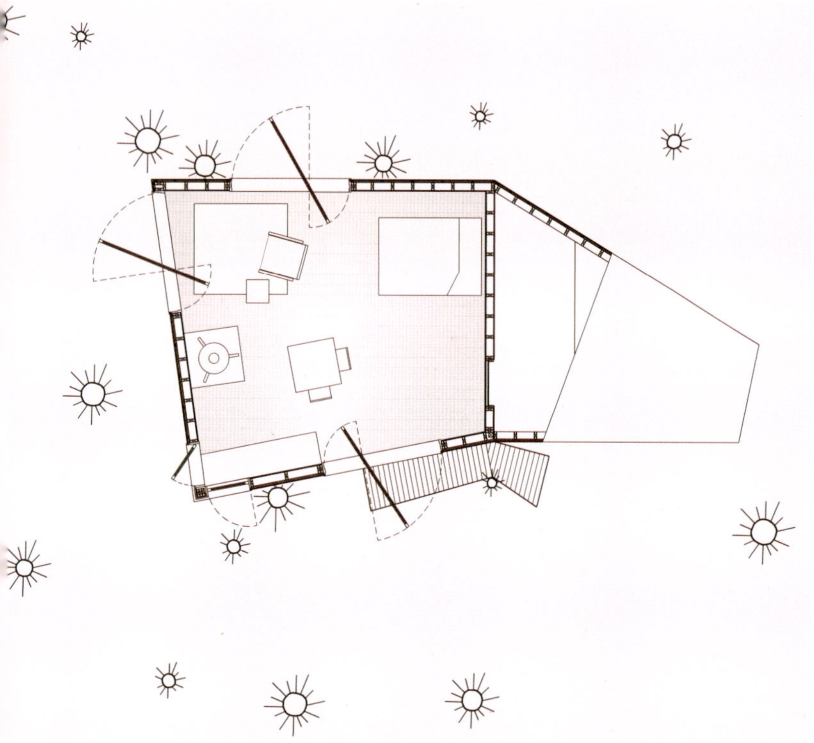

VILLA J

Vättlefjäll, Gothenburg, Sweden, 2020

SAGA KARLSSON AND EDOUARD BOISSE, *Olofstorp, Sweden*

VÄTTLEFJÄLL IS A NATURE RESERVE located about 30 minutes from the city of Gothenburg. Also called the Villa Jägersro, this residence contrasts with its natural setting but means to take it in as much as possible. Built on a sloped 2.3-square-acre (9,200-square-meter) site, the 2,045-square-foot (190-square-meter) house is reached via a wooden trellis corridor that leads down from a parking area. Visitors see views of a small lake below through large windows in the front façade that "blur the boundary between inside and out." The architects explain, "Inspired from the geometric rationality of a Roman architectural loggia, which acts as both practical and functional, Villa Jägersro's facade towards the lake re-creates the loggia." The square-plan house has an inner courtyard meaning that residents are surrounded by the presence of nature. The entrance, kitchen, dining, and living areas are situated to the front with the lake view, while the private areas—bedrooms and bathrooms, are to the back, more integrated to the forest setting. The architects explain, "An early sketch envisioned the house as an open and transparent glass volume inspired by a '60s Californian residence, which plays with the boundary of external and internal. However, after architects and homeowners Karlsson and Boisse first camped on site and saw the thriller *Signs* (Mel Gibson, Joaquin Phoenix, 2002), their sketches developed and produced the thick walls providing safety in the dark and wild environment." The architects have chosen an orthogonal form covered in wood painted matte black that is in willful contrast to the natural environment, or perhaps as they would explain, this austerity of form and color makes it easier to observe and be absorbed by nature. The lighter, tan and gray palette of the interiors emphasizes the light that comes in through the generous glazed surfaces, but here too a minimal intent is made clear—furnishings are quite "bare," and the resident is left to contemplate nature.

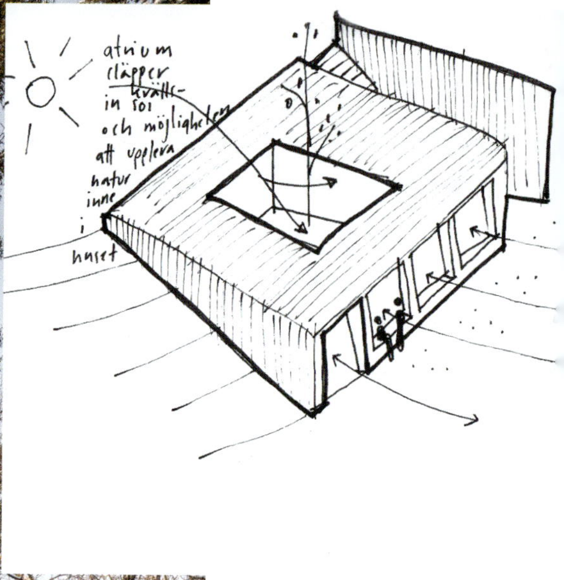
atrium
släpper
kvälls-
in sol
och möjligheten
att uppleva
natur
inne
i
huset

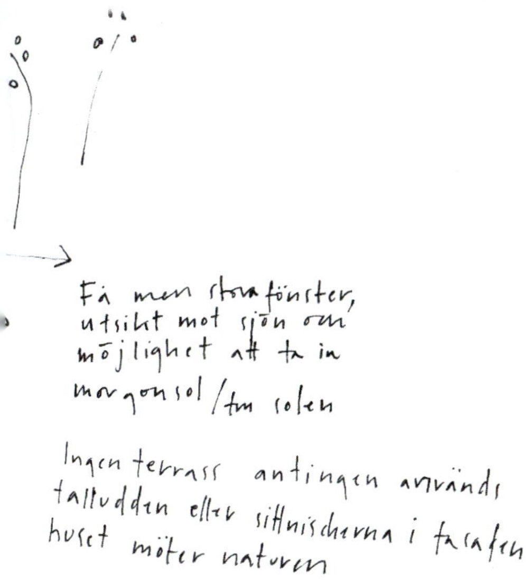
Få men stora fönster,
utsikt mot sjön om
möjlighet att ta in
morgonsol/fm solen
Ingen terrass antingen används
talludden eller sittnischerna i fasaden
huset möter naturen

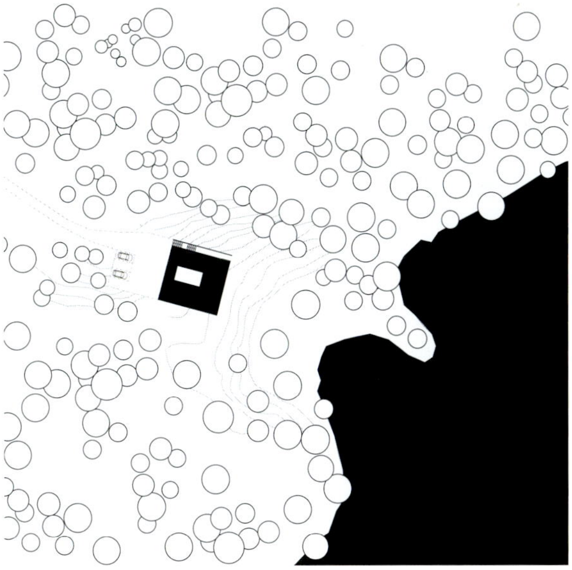

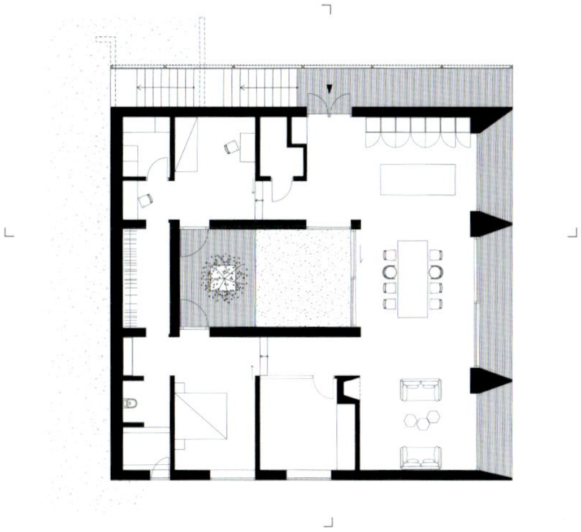

The MONOCLE Book of Gentle Living
Pierre Yovanovitch

opposite

Interiors are furnished in a simple way, with an emphasis on wood.

right

This view of the kitchen area reveals a minimal presence of furnishings and an emphasis on the large glazed opening.

MAXON HOUSE AND STUDIO

Carnation, Washington, United States, 2016/2022

TOM KUNDIG –
OLSON KUNDIG ARCHITECTS, *Seattle*

BUILT IN A FORMER Weyerhaeuser tree farm, the Maxon House and Studio were both designed and built successively by Tom Kundig, lead architect of Olson Kundig. The house, completed in 2016, has a floor area of 3,200 square feet (297 square meters). The more unusual studio was finished in 2022. It offers 300 square feet (28 square meters) of extra space that literally rolls 110 feet (33 meters) away from the house on railway tracks. A fire pit is located at the mid-point of the route, and the end is literally in the forest. The two-story structure is clad in Corten steel and glass and was the architect's response to the desire of the client, Lou Maxon, to have an isolated place to work on his 41.5-acre (16.8-hectare) property. Steel cables and track spikes found on the site also contributed to the decision to play on local railway heritage. The client served as the general contractor for the project and actively participated in the elaboration of the railway metaphor for his moving studio. The architect is known for including movable elements in his designs, but the Maxon Studio takes this interest to a new level. A control panel from a Burlington Northern locomotive was adapted to the control of the movements of the studio. In a bow to more contemporary Japanese technology, the studio has a stabilizing bar to keep it from tipping over in the case of an earthquake. A desk looks out from the studio to the forest, and a library is located on the upper level, which is reached via a steel ladder but is also served by a dumbwaiter. Because of a steep slope in the site, the main house is cantilevered, and the construction of the rail line required excavation and reinforcement of the route. The property is located about 27 miles (43 kilometers) to the east of Seattle and has views of the Tolt River Valley. The location and the orientation of the main house maximize views of the valley, although trees were left as undisturbed as possible. A similarity of materials and spirit unites the house to the studio; both are immersed in nature and yet offer privacy and comfort of a unique kind.

MAJAMAJA

Vuorilahdenniemi, Helsinki, Finland, 2022

PEKKA LITTOW, LITTOW ARCHITECTES,
Helsinki / Paris

THESE 253-SQUARE-FOOT (23.5-square-meter) cabins are made with prefabricated wooden elements. They feature off-grid technology including energy storage and a closed-circuit wastewater treatment system that is integrated in the prefabricated sanitary module. Solar panels and fuel cells are part of the design. Natural gas described as "non-polluting" is used for heating. The structures can be readily dismantled and moved to isolated sites. The architect explains, "Majamaja is a concrete response to the global trend towards sustainable construction and living. This project is inspired by life in the Finnish archipelago, its traditional habitat, its human-sized buildings, and its way of life in which man is in harmony with nature. In accordance with these principles, the project is intended to be global." The modular nature of the system allows for several units to be grouped together, and if necessary, connected to local networks. A dedicated company, Majamaja was created in Paris and Helsinki in 2017. This project is one of many initiatives worldwide that seek to address ecological issues in a responsible way, but also to permit truly off-grid living in remote locations. In recent years, new technologies have allowed off-grid homes to evolve to the point where modern comfort is now part of the equation. As described, the "basic electrical equipment" for these houses includes lights, a refrigerator, a microwave, a TV, and even optional air-conditioning. Although it is permitted to ask if air-conditioning and ecological responsibility can really go hand in hand, the concept here is one of reconciling the desire to be cut off from urban stress while still having a modern place to live. The small size and foldout furnishings of these cabins do imply a modest way of life, which may be as important in recovering ecological balance as sophisticated means to provide modern comfort as close as possible to the goal of sustainability.

previous

Relatively dark interiors contrast with the generous view of the outside from the kitchen seating area. Left, a small bed folds out.

right

A bed beneath the ceiling of the house above a door open to the water.

THE HERMITAGE

Val Trebbia, Italy, 2021

LLABB, *Genoa*

THIS 129-SQUARE-FOOT (12-square-meter) cabin was self-built by the studio on a natural site during a two-week workshop. Okoume plywood was chosen because of its superior weather resistance, but this wood (*Aucoumea klaineana*) is found in the Congo, Gabon, and Equatorial Guinea. The modular design can be used as "a studio, a retreat, a tearoom, or a guesthouse." The architects at LLABB began their practice in 2013 by creating a carpentry workshop in a garage, whence their interest in this type of project. Thcy cite Japanese teahouses and Swedish cabins as sources of information for this off-grid structure that was built in a remote area between Liguria and Emilia-Romagna. Set on a steep slope, the house is approached from the rear via a small footbridge. It has a plywood interior with a fully glazed wall facing southeast. One of the four windows opens to a small terrace suspended above the forest floor and taking in the generous view. The structure is anchored in the sandstone of the site with four 23.6-by-23.6-inch (60-by-60-centimeter) bases and four wooden pillars. A small foldout bed above a sofa and a little bathroom with a compostable toilet are part of the design. The plywood walls, floor, and ceiling were pre-assembled, and a corrugated metal sheet roof was added together with two photovoltaic panels. The architects emphasize that "the structure can easily be connected to a sewer system and water supply." The blocky appearance of the cabin corresponds to its intentional modesty and sustainable design and construction. Given its very light footprint, this structure can be readily removed with little or no damage to the site. It does not seek to achieve higher levels of comfort but nonetheless offers an attractive and relatively inexpensive alternative to other off-grid designs that aspire to greater comfort.

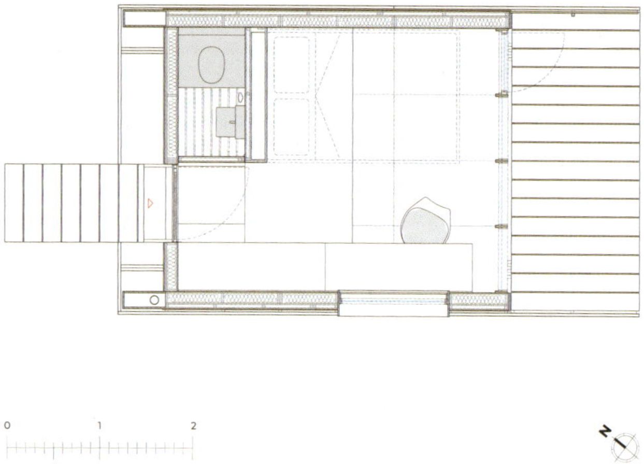
0
1
2
0.5
N

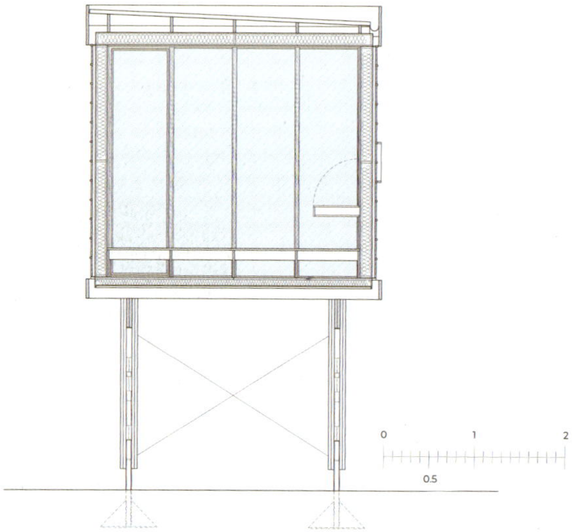
0
1
2
0.5

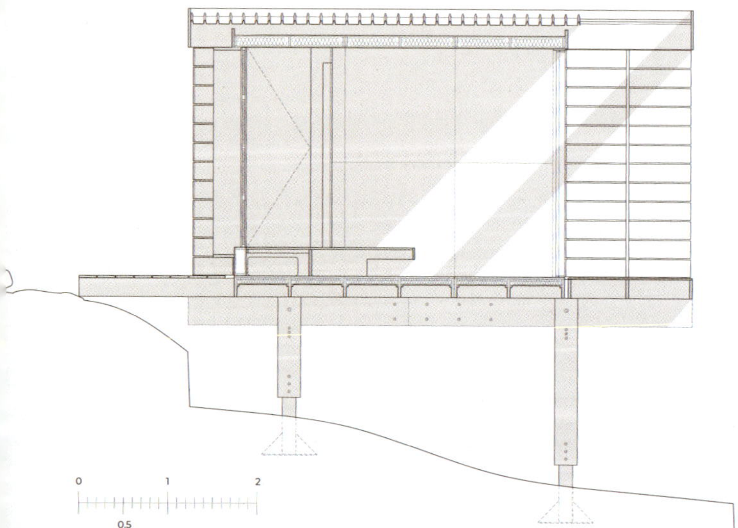
0
1
2
0.5

BACK COUNTRY HOUSE

Puhoi, New Zealand, 2016

LTD ARCHITECTURAL DESIGN STUDIO, *Auckland*

ALTHOUGH IT ALSO HAS A PARTIALLY covered terrace, this house basically has a single-slope roof, which creates room for the upstairs master bedroom. The upstairs bed is suspended beneath the slope of the roof, which has a large window providing ample views of the night sky. Other spaces for eating and living are on the main level together with a generous wooden deck that has a fireplace and twin bathtubs—usually covered by a low table. There are also two smaller bedrooms and a bathroom on the ground floor. The full glazed surfaces of the living area fold open to make the interior contiguous with this terrace. The architects emphasize that the spaces of the house are shared as opposed to being private. Locally sourced Macrocarpa (*Hesperocyparis macrocarpa*) is used both inside and out together with some galvanized corrugated iron. Passive heating and high-performance insulation further reduce the environmental impact of this hut. The architects were also attentive to interior design. They write, "The main palette is two-tone, with the warmth of the oil-blonded Macrocarpa off-setting the starkness of the matte-white surfaces; meanwhile matte-black light fittings work together with the joinery to accent the scheme. The simplicity of the palette provides a sense of calm, which works as a welcome backdrop to the sometimes-chaotic days of young family life." Cabinetry and other furnishings are most often integrated, like the kitchen cabinetry, or tucked into ancillary spaces—making the whole appear to be neat and spacious. The house built in Puhoi, about 31 miles (50 kilometers) north of Auckland, has an area of 1,765 square feet (164 square meters).

Laney

10

BLOCK HOUSE

Somerset, UK, 2021

MATERIAL CULTURES, *London*

THIS 969-SQUARE-FOOT (90-square-meter) house built on the site of a former hermitage on an estate in Somerset sought to have the lowest embodied carbon imprint possible. This was done by using locally sourced timber, hempcrete, and wood-fiber insulation. Hempcrete is made with lime, sand, or pozzolans and is ten times stronger than concrete and six times lighter. Set on flint foundations and placed to avoid cutting mature trees, "Block House is a prototypical, experimental building which demonstrates low-carbon construction is not only possible but can also create beautiful places to live." The building is clad in locally sourced larch and cedar shingles, and the terrace was made with a series of oak columns. As the designers say, the structure is "effectively compostable." Clay-based paints were chosen for the interior "for their breathability and lack of volatile organic compounds." The hermitage that had been located nearby until it was destroyed by a falling tree in 2018 had a concrete slab foundation that the architects removed to avoid damaging surface roots of nearby trees. Although the description of the architects puts emphasis on the ecological credentials of this small house, it is both elegant and comfortable in appearance. Photographed just as it was being completed, the house is made to weather and blend into its surroundings. The careful attention paid to embodied carbon, sustainability, and the recyclable aspect of the entire project means that this is not what might be called a high-tech approach to ecological concerns. It is instead a return to many of the methods and materials that were used for centuries in this and other places. Before global transport of materials was even imagined, houses had to be built with readily available materials. This is clearly a relatively low-budget project, but that too proves just how it is possible to respect nature and the environment while still having a modern place to live.

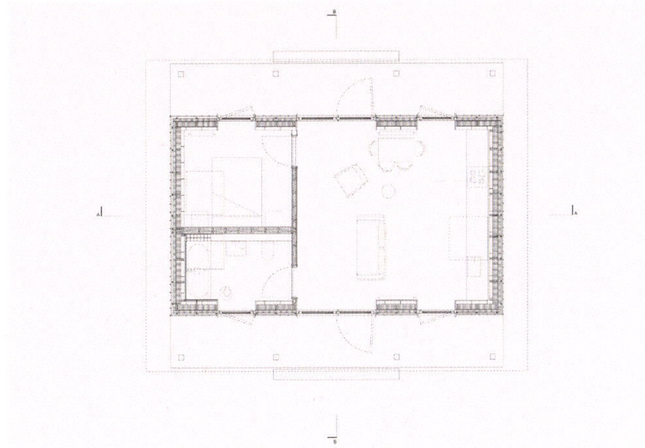

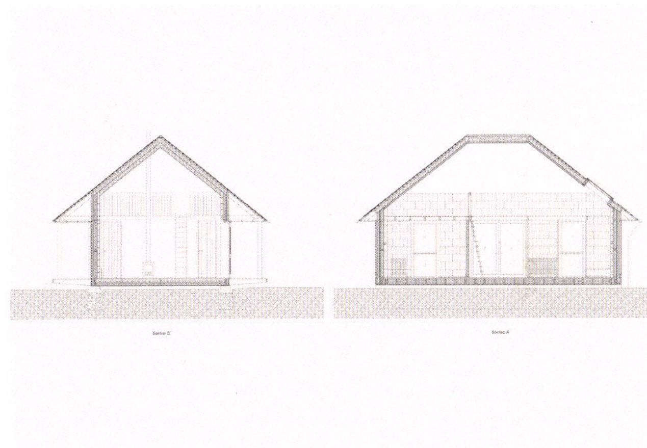

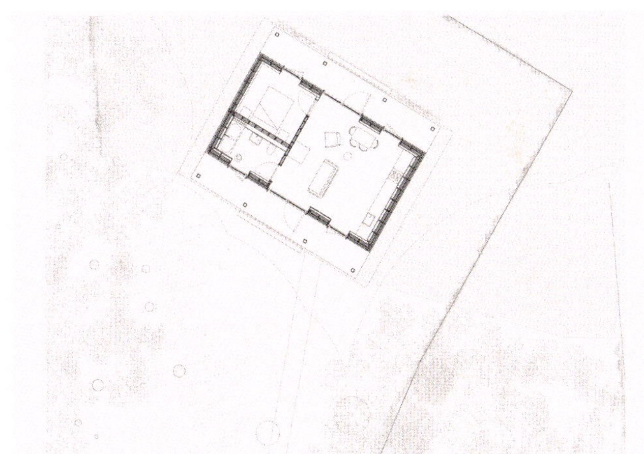

left and opposite

The simple materials and detailing create a light, modern atmosphere, with a wood-burning stove visible.

GLASS VILLA ON THE LAKE

Lechlade, UK, 2018

MECANOO ARCHITECTEN, *Delft, The Netherlands*

THE LAKES BY YOO IS AN estate in the Cotswalds where luxury homes have been developed. Mecanoo participated in the project with this 6,458-square-foot (600-square-meter) three-story villa a level below grade with a cinema, game room, bar, and wellness/spa areas. There is an 861-square-foot (80-square-meter) roof terrace and a 1,894-square-foot (176-square-meter) ground-floor terrace. The architects state, "The guiding design principle was to create a house that combines transparency with sustainability, forging a strong relationship between the villa and the landscape. The harmony between landscape and interior, architecture and nature, was a key design determinant, particularly regarding sight lines, materials, colors, and lighting. The house is designed from inside out, creating uninterrupted views to the surrounding nature while providing shelter and intimacy." The composition of the plan is strictly rectangular. The proximity of both vegetation and the extensive glazing of the house give it a sense of privacy and intimacy despite its large scale. Because it projects out over the edge of the lake, the house almost gives the impression of being a floating object in this setting. Black metal finishing and white surfaces combine to confirm the geometric rigor of the house but also to call more attention to the green environment and the neighboring water. The Rotterdam practice Mecanoo is of course known for much larger public projects like the Tainan Public Library (Taiwan), Library of Birmingham (UK), or the European Investment Bank (Luxembourg, ongoing). This house has a feeling that may well evoke larger architecture; it is closely related to nature but also strongly geometric and machined in its presence.

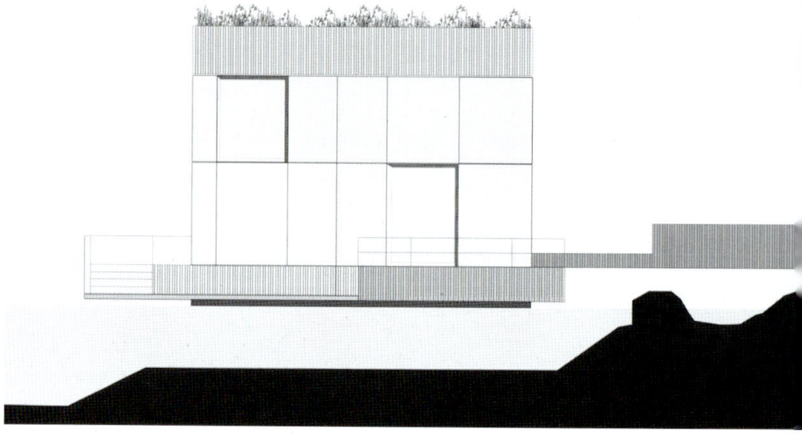

HOUSE IN THE TREES

Sierra Nevada, Curacautin, Chile, 2023

MAX NÚÑEZ BANCALARI +
STEFANO ROLLA, *Santiago*

CURACAUTIN IS A TOWN of about 16,000 people located in a volcanic region at the foot of the Andes in central Chile. More precisely, this house is on the northern slope of the Sierra Nevada range near the Conquillio National Park. With a floor area of 1,184 square feet (110 square meters), the house was designed to have the least possible impact on the natural surroundings. The architect explains that the upper level of the house is lifted off the ground by a largely prefabricated structure that resembles a bridge, with a perimeter lattice beam. Given the relatively remote location, the prefabrication system allowed this residence to be built by a small team in a short period of time. Despite its unusual elevation scheme, the upper part of the house suggests an A-frame design. The compact private area of the house is on the main floor with a large space for the kitchen and living space above, set nearly 40 feet (12 meters) above the ground. The overhanging volume of the house serves to protect the ground area from rain or accumulations of snow. The architect states, "This space gives a vantage point on the surroundings, as a watchtower detached from the ground, with a close relation to nature and the pass of time." He compares the house to a "tree-like structure with a central trunk enclosed in translucent glass." This is the entrance level where the residents can store winter equipment in a region that is known for winter trekking. Max Núñez Bancalari, working here with the Italian architect Stefano Rolla, born in 1976 in Milan, who is also part of the team Valdivieso-Rolla in Santiago, has shown a mastery for the creation of very contemporary houses in sometimes extreme environments.

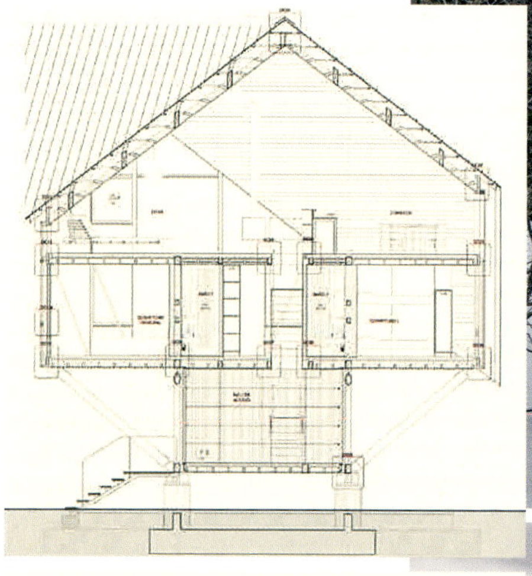

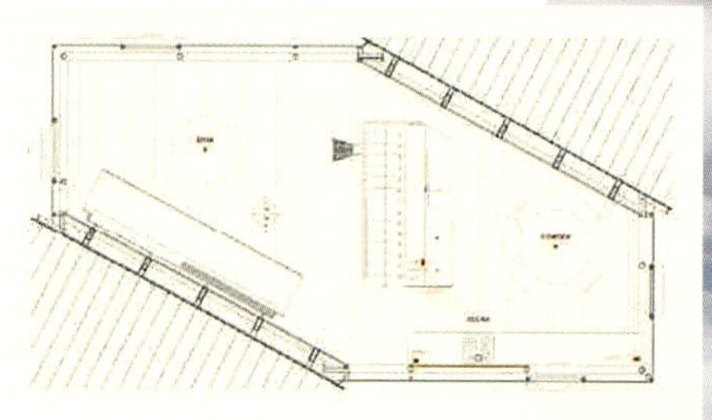

right

The surprising forms of the house are visible in the drawings above and in the photos on this page.

opposite

Skis and boots are left on the ground floor for residents who climb the steep stairs into the house.

CASA OCHOALCUBO

Los Vilos, Coquimbo Region, Chile, 2021

MAX NÚÑEZ ARQUITECTOS, *Santiago*

LOS VILOS IS LOCATED 140 miles (225 kilometers) northwest of Santiago on the Pacific coast of Chile. This new house is part of the Ochoalcubo/Ochoquebradas development, where eight Chilean architects and eight Japanese architects were invited to design a collection of sixteen houses. Houses had already been completed in this series by the Pritzker Architecture Prize winners Ryue Nishizawa (SANAA) and Alejandro Aravena (Elemental). Like the earlier houses, the Casa Ochoalcubo has remarkable views of the ocean. Max Núñez Bancalari states, "This coastline is renowned for its rich marine-coastal biodiversity and the presence of endemic species, creating a unique landscape that needs to be preserved." Rather than being perched on rocks like the Nishizawa project, this residence is in dunes, and is perceived as a "flat surface that harmoniously integrates with its surroundings, ensuring unobstructed views of the horizon and the sea." The architect imagined a superposition of three types of curves starting with the foundations. A second curve delineates the perimeter of the enclosed spaces. The third curvature is the roof with extended eaves that shelter the terraces below. A sculptural stairway leading to an enclosed courtyard marks the roof. This entry through the roof emphasizes the low-lying nature of the architecture and brings visitors and residents into a remarkable (curving) panorama of the ocean coast of Los Vilos. Max Núñez Bancalari explains, "This juxtaposition of layouts creates an irregular edge that offers different views and situations, blurring the transition between the interior and the exterior. This 'fluid' geometry establishes impossible relationships at multiple scales: with the landscape and the undulating contours of the coastal edge, as well as with the shells of bivalve mollusks found by the shore, from which the house borrows its form."

LAKESIDE HOUSE

Yamanashi, Japan, 2015

SHINICHI OGAWA & ASSOCIATES, *Hiroshima / Tokyo*

BORN IN 1955 IN Yamaguchi Prefecture, Shinichi Ogawa graduated from Nihon University College of Art (Tokyo, 1978). He also studied with the architecture faculty of Washington State University (1977). He lived in New York as an overseas artist trainee under the auspices of the Japanese Agency of Cultural Affairs. There, he worked in the offices of Paul Rudolph (1984) and Arquitectonica (1985) and established his own firm, Shinichi Ogawa & Associates, in 1986. He has developed a strongly minimalist style that is seen to its best advantage in the Lakeside House published here. This is a one-story 2,034-square-foot (189-square-meter) weekend house designed with a steel structure. It is set on a 13,045-square-foot (1,212-square-meter) site and located on the shores of Lake Kawaguchiko near Mount Fuji. The low rectangular volume measures 98 by 21 feet (30 by 6.3 meters), with the longer side turned toward the lake "to provide a full view from all rooms." The house has a white concrete base and a fully glazed, very simple interior—a "neutral space without any decorative elements opposite nature." The main living area and the bedrooms are fully glazed on three sides. Even the hot tub has a generous view to the lake and countryside. Existing trees on the site, a Japanese maple (*Acer palmatum*) and a large Zelkova (*Zelkova serrata*), were preserved. Although very modern, minimalist forms may be in strong contrast to a natural setting like this one, the architect clearly feels that this house and its situation encourage, rather than discourage, contact with nature. He writes, "The surface of a lake begins to move with wind and shines. We planned a house intended for the enjoyment of nature of the surrounding environment. . . . This architecture is a wonderful place that provides a feeling of changing nature in all seasons. It is filled with refreshing light in the morning, and it becomes a space colored by the glowing sunset when the reflecting shimmer on the lake surface reaches the interior space." Lake Kawaguchiko is one of the so-called Fuji Five Lakes. The area can be reached by train or bus from Tokyo and is about 63 miles (102 kilometers) southwest of the capital.

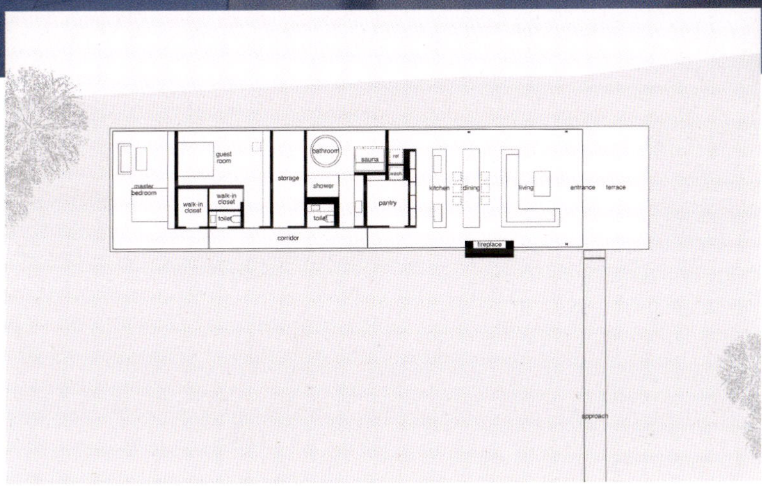

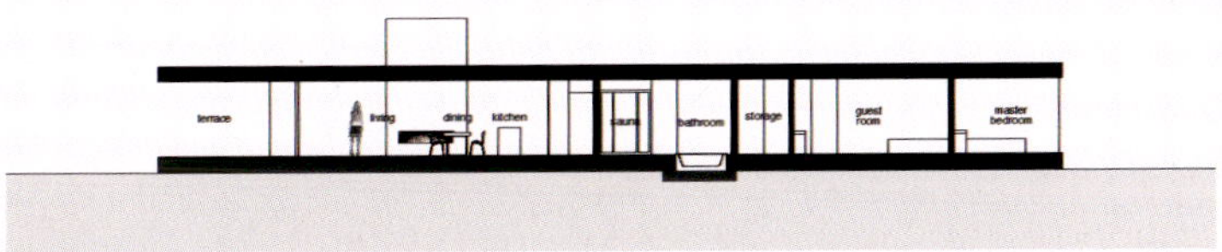

section 01

section 02

opposite and above

The house demonstrates an extreme minimalism and lightness that privileges the lakeside setting.

left

In the plan, the house forms a long narrow rectangle. The section drawings are equally reduced in their complexity to leave only what is essential.

COSTA RICA TREEHOUSE

Santa Teresa, Costa Rica, 2017

OLSON KUNDIG, *Seattle*

SANTA TERESA IS LOCATED on the Pacific in western Costa Rica. The architects explain, "Costa Rica Treehouse is inspired by the jungle of its densely forested site on the Pacific coast of Costa Rica. Built entirely of locally harvested teak wood, the retreat engages with the jungle at each of its three levels: the ground floor opens to the forest floor, the middle level is nestled within the trees, and the top level rises above the tree canopy with views of the surf at nearby Playa Hermosa beach." Although teak is not a local species, it grows readily in Costa Rica, and the architects were able to obtain it there. A 3.5-kilowatt photovoltaic array and a rainwater collection system participate in a largely passive energy system that means the house, built for clients who are environmentalists, can be entirely off-grid and takes advantage of the warm climate of Costa Rica. It is, in fact, described as "carbon positive." As is often the case in Kundig's houses, the residence can be closed with an operable wood shutter system when the clients are away. The house has an interior area of 2,140 square feet (199 square meters) and outdoor decks that add another 624 square feet (58 square meters) of space as well as a swimming pool. The architect Tom Kundig states, "The project has an intentionally small footprint and is quite tall—this allowed us to maintain a light influence on the site while engaging with the natural landscape in different ways on all three levels of the house." This house was the winner of a 2022 AIA Housing Award for one- and two-family residences. The jury statement for the award read in part, "A beautiful lantern in the jungle, this design is a celebration of time-honored craft and materials. It touches the earth lightly and with respect. A masterfully simple home that elevates shelter to a poetic level."

HOUSE FOR A DRUMMER

Kärna, Västra Götaland, Sweden, 2016

OLSSON LYCKEFORS ARKITEKTUR, *Gothenburg*

LOCATED ON THE WEST COAST of Sweden half an hour north of Gothenburg, this house was inspired in its form by old farm buildings that were previously on the site. The architect states, "The new house is a straightforward warehouse-inspired volume with a distinct framing and with large barnyard doors covering the windows facing west, all painted in traditional Swedish Falu red color." The house basically forms a two-level red wooden cube, but there is a third intermediate level where the drums of the client were placed as well as the two small bedrooms of the children. The intermediate level and the varying ceiling heights increase the spatial complexity and interest of the house. The client was a single father of two children who wanted the residence to blend into the site as much as possible while still retaining its own identity. A concrete floor on the ground level continues smoothly to a rectangular exterior terrace. An "open section" concept allows the interior spaces to interact and flow into each other. The living and dining spaces are on the ground floor along with a niche bed that was imagined for the children, or as a place to read. Plywood was used for the ceilings, exposed beams, built-in furniture, including the bookshelf, and for the stairway. The kitchen is finished in dark gray fiberboard. The living room reaches up higher than the other ground-floor space, making room for the intermediate level. A small balcony and the master bedroom are located at the top of the house. The house has a floor area of 1,754 square feet (163 square meters). Andreas Lyckefors, the architect of this house, was born in Sweden in 1975. He studied at Chalmers University of Technology and then at the Technical University of Delft, where he received his master's degree. He worked at the Swedish firm Wingårdhs in Gothenburg and with OMA/Rem Koolhaas in Rotterdam amongst other firms before founding his own practice, Olsson Lyckefors, in 2004.

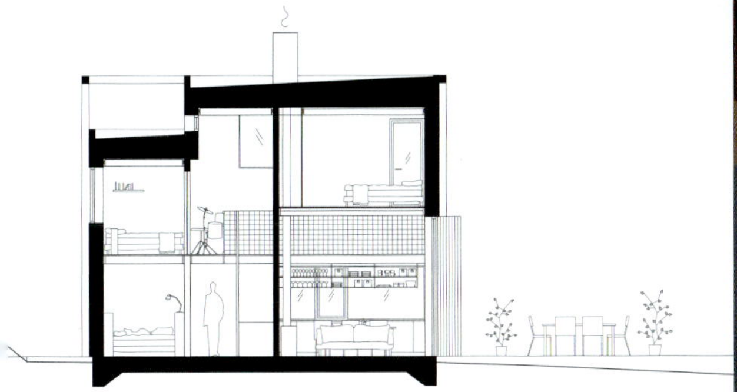

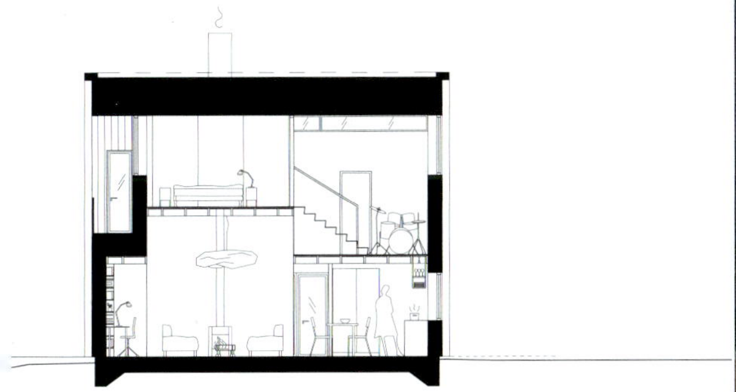

opposite

The house opens to the environment but also has interior volumes that penetrate each other and create a feeling of communication.

this page

Above, two section drawings and a main floor plan. Right, a chair in a space beneath the stairway with the bookshelves also visible.

CASA AGUACATES

Valle de Bravo, Mexico, 2020

FRANCISCO PARDO, *Mexico City*

ALTHOUGH IT IS INTENDED as a weekend home for residents of Mexico City, Casa Aguacates is large —4,757 square feet (442 square meters). Set in an avocado field at the edge of forest land, the house is in good part buried in the site. At its rear, the house opens into a green field. It is entered from an outdoor staircase that descends from the southern end of the buried building. As seen from above, only four skylights betray the presence of a residence. According to the architect, the fact that the client enjoys hang-gliding made it important to blend the roof into the landscape as much as possible. The living areas—including the kitchen and dining space—are in the center of the plan, with a studio and the master bedroom to one side and two guest rooms at the opposite end. A sunken garden was created near the living room. Concrete walls and some surfaces that are covered in stucco participate in a design that is intended to be simple to maintain. Recuperated pine formwork for the in-situ concrete was used for interior partitions and for a small, separate cabin. This house, built in concrete that is mostly below grade, with a green roof, clearly integrates itself into the natural setting and inevitably is energy efficient, though the local climate is rarely very cold or warm (43 to 82°F / 6 to 28°C). Subterranean dwelling goes back almost as far as the first shelters—caves, for example. This is a sophisticated take on a very old way of living for clients who wanted the exterior appearance of the house to not make a very visible statement.

left

The staircase enters the partially buried volume from above, making the house blend into its site.

opposite

The low-lying house and its entry stairway seen from above.

MAGNOLIA NET ZERO CABIN

Nederland, Colorado, United States, 2022

MICHAEL QUIRK DESIGN, *Boulder, Colorado*

THE VERY SMALL HOUSE (120 square feet, 11 square meters) is located on a 5-acre (2-hectare) site, a parcel belonging to friends who had access to water and sewage treatment. It was built with birch plywood, reused cedar shiplap siding, shou sugi ban charred pine, reused windows, a wood-burning stove, hempcrete, solar panels, reused bricks, metal panels that had been furnished as architectural samples, and certified Douglas fir framing. The charred pine was charred according to a Japanese method to prevent pests and improve the durability of wood used in construction. The architect explains, "This project is a showcase for carbon negative materials, combined with Passive House design techniques." Well insulated and airtight, the building envelope is quite efficient, and the use of solar energy means that it is a net-zero building. Again, according to Michael Quirk, "The hemp insulation and wood structure and finishes mean that the building is storing more carbon than is embodied in the materials used. Although that is the main goal of the project, it also is successful in addressing other aspects of sustainability like reuse and justice. . . . Lastly, the cabin has provided inexpensive housing for me and my girlfriend in a place where the housing crisis excludes many people from the community. Building infill alternative housing like this can be a solution to the lack of affordable housing for all kinds of people."

CASA PATIOS

Ranchos San José, Lasso, Cotopaxi, Ecuador, 2019

RAMA ESTUDIO, *Quito*

THE HOUSE WAS BUILT in a rural environment and was imagined from the outset as being buried in the ground. Solid stone walls support the inclined roof, which is divided in two and slants down to the earth. The two parts of the metal roof are respectively 33 and 39 feet (10 and 12 meters) in length and just 0.15 inches (4 millimeters) thick, coated with 10 inches (25 centimeters) of stone and soil for the vegetation that covers it. Two patios, one on each side, extend from the central section where the roofs part, and where the main social space is located. An "open-covered" space between the roofs is the location of a barbecue that links to the kitchen. Traditional bahareque panels, made of bamboo and earth, divide the interior spaces. The architects explain, "Bahareque improves the thermal and acoustic conditions of the house, while its texture and color reinforce the intention of generating a discrete object in the landscape." The outer limits of the house are defined by a series of columns of solid eucalyptus, alternating with panels of bahareque and glass screens that admit light, and entrance to the house. The architects state, "From the beginning, a discrete project was proposed, which integrates itself into the environment, which does not stand out on the ground, where the vegetation prevails over the built space. This landscape strategy is the one that governs the entire area, an idea that suggests that the landscape surrounds the house. The vegetation starts at the ground and grows over the house through the roof, overflows and falls covering the stone walls." This house seems like a hybrid emerging somewhere between rural architecture and sophisticated modern means. The architects do not emphasize the environmental qualities of the design—in a sense they don't need to; both the materials and aspects such as the green roof speak for themselves. The residents here live with and in nature.

previous

The materials and form of the house are simple and direct with ample openings and a dominance of wood surfaces.

opposite and right

A wood-burning stove sites in the double-height living and dining space with its generous horizontal, full-height glazing.

NIDOS HOUSE

Valle de Bravo, Mexico, 2021

CLAUDIA RODRÍGUEZ + ROZANA MONTIEL ESTUDIO DE ARQUITECTURA, *Mexico City*

BUILT IN AN ECOLOGICAL RESERVE called El Peñón, the Nidos House is in part suspended from load-bearing walls and touches the ground only in an area of 108 square feet (10 square meters). Intended to bring together the interiors with broad views of the green exterior, the house is compared to bird nests, hence its name Nidos. The architects explain that the house includes three main areas—the entrance, parking, and service space—the central section, which takes the form of an elevated rectangular volume, and the third that includes bungalows for guests and a vegetable garden. The architects explain, "The house is a concrete monolith, visually warm, because of its wood-colored finish that was given to the cement both inside and outside." The roofs of the house collect rainwater and direct into a subterranean cistern with a capacity of 26,400 gallons (100,000 liters). Excess water is used for the gardens, while wastewater is treated directly on-site. This is a large residence with a main pavilion measuring 3,713 square feet (345 square meters), and visitor bungalows with an area of 1,227 square feet (114 square meters). Although rectilinear in plan and section, the house is surrounded by lush vegetation and makes use of wood and stone to relate the interiors to the exterior. Clearly this is an architecture of warm climates, but it does represent a very seductive way to create a relation and an engagement between interior and exterior, nature and built form. Claudia Rodríguez was born in Mexico City in 1972. She graduated in architecture and urbanism from the Universidad Iberoamericana in Mexico City in 1996 and studied for a master's degree in architectural theory and criticism at the Polytechnic University of Catalonia (Spain, 1999). Rozana Montiel was born in Mexico City in 1972. She has a master of arts in architectural theory and criticism from the Polytechnic University of Catalonia (Spain, 2000) and a bachelor of arts in architecture and urban planning from the Universidad Iberoamericana (Mexico, 1998).

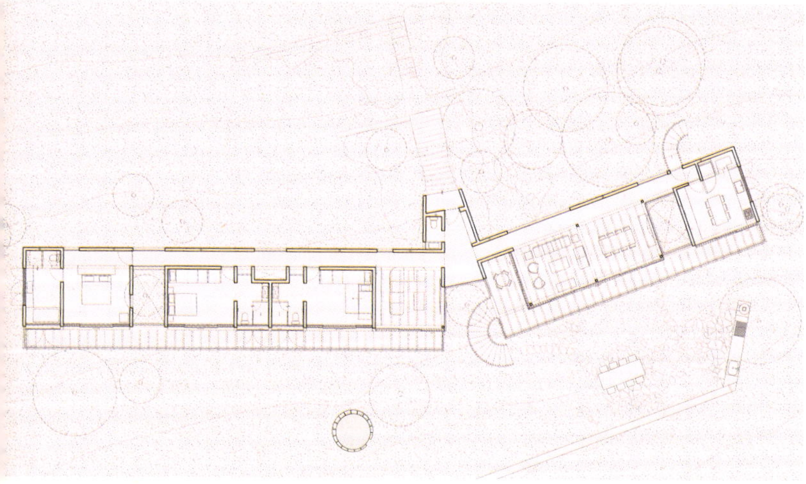

above and right

A perspective drawing and a site plan show the angled wings of the house. The curving stairway rises to the elevated main floor.

PENINSULA HOUSE

Stockholm Archipelago, Sweden, 2021

RICKARD ROTSTEIN, *Stockholm*

BUILT ON A CLIFF ON A ROCKY, wooded site, this 1,400-square-foot (130-square-meter) house offers views of the Stockholm Archipelago and is near a protected nature zone. Neither the cliff itself nor trees on the site were disturbed in any significant way, rather the plan was created around what existed, and what was possible without heavy construction. The site of the house covers a total of 32,291 square feet (3,000 square meters). It was built with locally sourced pine. The façades are in local spruce, which has been coated with tar, linseed oil, and balsamic turpentine. The architect built this house as his own summer residence. It is located about an hour and a half from Stockholm, where he works. The kitchen, on the ground level, is next to the entrance. A dining area is contiguous with the living room in an open plan, and both open through a fully glazed façade to a very spacious wooden deck. The space visible from the entrance extends just under 65 feet (20 meters). A bathroom and two bedrooms complete the level, with just the loft that the architect uses to work and a terrace above. A fireplace is set near the steps that lead up to the loft. The ceilings of the house are in matt-lacquered OSB board, and the floors in whitened oak. Contemporary and vintage Scandinavian art and furnishings are placed to make a comfortable and attractive environment. The architect does not emphasize the ecological credentials of this house, but using local wood (and labor) as well as carefully protecting trees and rocks, or relying on a wood-burning chimney for heat, are all significant aspects in affirming the sustainability of architecture. Nor have any of these precautions made the house less attractive or comfortable.

opposite

The existing topography and vegetation were a guide for the design and placement of the house.

right and following

Part of the volume is lifted off the ground, offering a better view of the water and the wooded site.

RIFUGIO

Val Bregaglia, Switzerland, 2014

HANS-JÖRG RUCH, *Saint-Moritz*

LOCATED NOT FAR from Stampa, the village of the Giacometti family in Lower Engadine, this is the house of the architect. Hans-Jörg Ruch and his wife collect works by the Giacometti family and others, and much of it is displayed in the gallery floors of this "refuge." It stands out strongly from its rural village environment, because of its form and because of its material—rough concrete outside and slightly smoother concrete inside. The roughness of the exterior surface is due to the addition of crushed stone, excavated from the site to the concrete mix. Watch towers were, of course, a feature of earlier architecture in this region, which is on the route between Italy and Austria, so the form is not an entirely unexpected one in this place. From the roof of the house, and from within, through large windows, residents can see the spectacular mountains of the Bregaglia Range. An outdoor stairway leads to this flat roof that is covered in very large stones. The formwork for the house was made with 10.6-inch-wide (27-centimeter) boards, which, according to the architect, "determines the whole geometry of the house." The rough boards used leave an imprint on the finished walls that makes them look "like carpenters' work." In an unexpected gesture, which is in keeping with the architecture itself, the doors are made with solid wood boards of the same width that have no frames—they simply fit into the concrete openings provided. Ruch and his son Andy, who is now taking over their firm, are known in Engadine for their sensitive renovations and updating of existing old structures—considering the materials and nature of the spaces, while still looking to create contemporary volumes, as they did, for example, in the case of the Tschudi Gallery in Zuoz. The Rifugio is a different matter—purely new and appearing like "a giant rock" out of its steep hillside site. This is a different approach to context than others seen in this volume. It has to do with contrast to an old farming environment, but also to proximity to the peaked granite mountains that rise from the foot of the Maloja Pass. Despite its relative isolation, Engadine is a place of culture and history—of art and architecture—and Ruch is very much a part of the contemporary scene there.

previous

The house is a testimony to the rugged beauty of the Bregaglia area of Engadine, near Stampa, the home of the Giacometti family.

left

The dwelling, which houses a substantial collection of the work of local artists, is entirely made of concrete and wood.

BARN CONVERSION

Praz-de-Fort, Valais, Switzerland, 2016

SAVIOZ FABRIZZI ARCHITECTES, *Sion*

THIS SMALL BARN, with a footprint of 700 square feet (65 square meters), was originally built in the second half of the nineteenth century not far from this site, in Saleinaz. The architects, who are based in the Valais region of Switzerland, created a new, independent structure inside the walls of the old barn. A bedroom and study area were placed in the upper part of the structure, with a view on the living and kitchen areas. The original barn doors were reused in a glazed form, while other openings were created in the originally closed building. The architects were, as usual, careful not to fundamentally disturb the nature of the building's facades. A concrete base was created along the lines of the original stone foundation of the building. In the formerly open space between the foundation and the upper wooden structure, the architects added a band of glazing that allows natural light to amply penetrate the space in the new base of the house. The new interior of the upper part of the 1,937-square-foot (180-square-meter) house was treated in a uniform manner with oak panels, while a more mineral approach was taken for the space in the base of the building. Laurent Savioz was born in 1976 and received his degree in architecture from the Haute École Spécialisée (HES) in Fribourg (1998). He worked in the office of Bonnard and Wœffray Architectes in Monthey, Switzerland (1999–2003), before co-founding Savioz Meyer Fabrizzi in Sion with François Meyer and Claude Fabrizzi in 2004. The current firm, created in 2005, is an association between Savioz and Claude Fabrizzi, born in 1975 in Sierre, and a graduate of the HES Fribourg (1995–98).

opposite and following

The architects have rendered the interior of the apparently old, traditional structure thoroughly modern, using wood and large glazed openings.

this page

Right, a section drawing and floor plans. Below, the kitchen and dining space, leading up the living area.

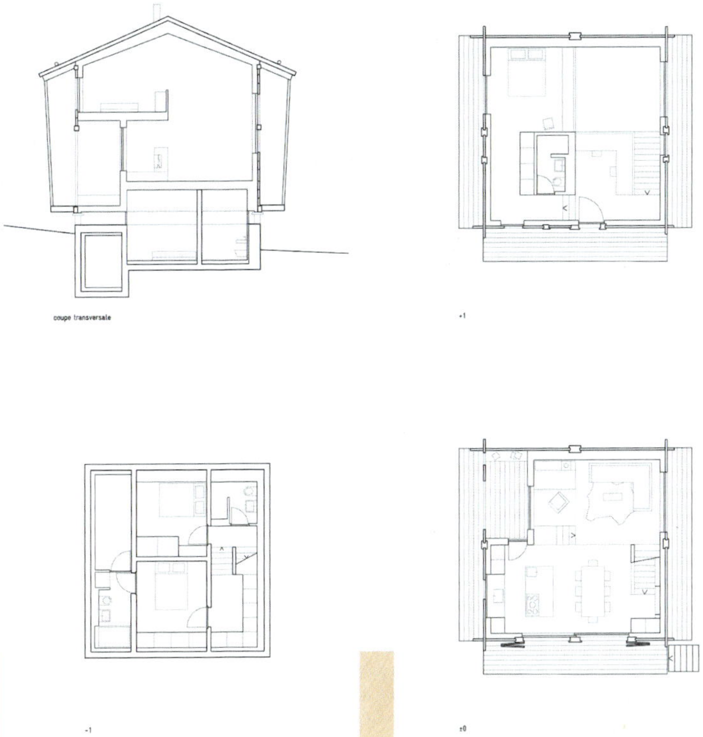

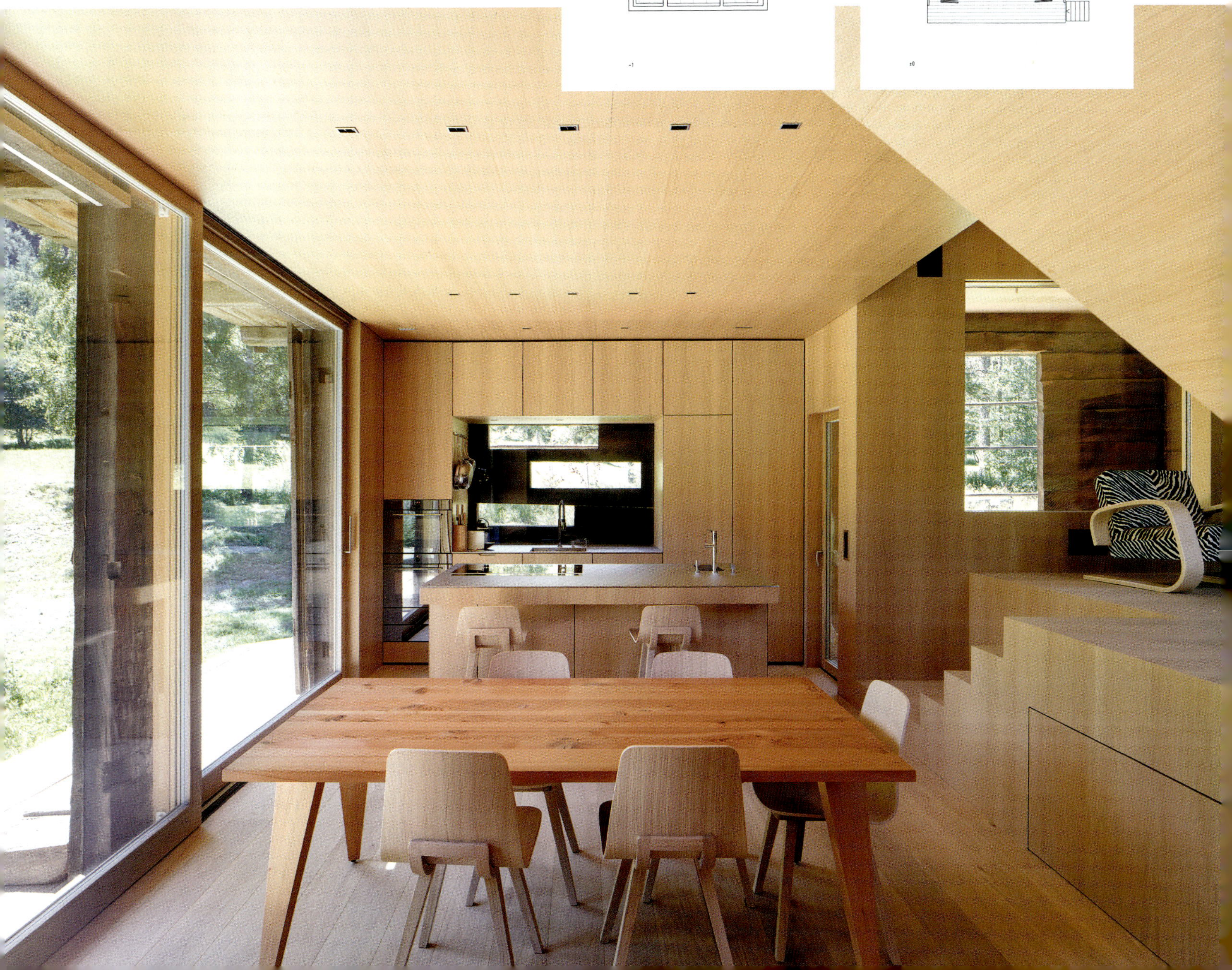

CAMPER HOUSE

Aposentillo, Chinandega, Nicaragua, 2022

DANIEL SERRANO, *Chinandega, Nicaragua*

DANIEL SERRANO, WHO IS FROM the Basq Guillermo Acuña ue region of Spain, studied architecture at the University of San Sebastián. He bought a camper in Oregon in 2019 and headed south, eventually to the Pan-American Highway with the idea of taking four months off to go surfing. He found a location in Nicaragua, near Chinandega on the Pacific Coast. He bought 27,986 square feet (2,600 square meters) of land there, installed his camper on the site, and began to work as an architect in the area. During the rainy season (May to October), he felt that the camper needed to be sheltered, and he added a slightly pitched corrugated steel roof. Using locally sourced wood, and metal joints from a welder in the area, he added a teak and fabric partition on a track in front of the camper and wood panel window coverings that are operated with a rope-and-pulley system. Night lighting is provided by hanging paper lanterns. Serrano and a friend put the camper up on stilts on a minimal concrete slab base. A teak bath was added, and the central dining and living space remained fully open to the garden. The architect rents the 237-square-foot (22-square-meter) house on Airbnb when he travels. "The intention of the Camper House," he says, "is to explore the essentials for a magical holiday shelter within a small budget, an experimental building that explores the romance of what is not needed in a house." This idea of a house may be better suited to a young surfer than to older persons, but it does show how a little ingenuity can change a basic camper into a kind of small paradise, given a location like this one on the Pacific shore where the temperatures hover around 86°F (30°C) all year long. Nearby Chinandega is the second-largest city in the country and is near the border with Honduras.

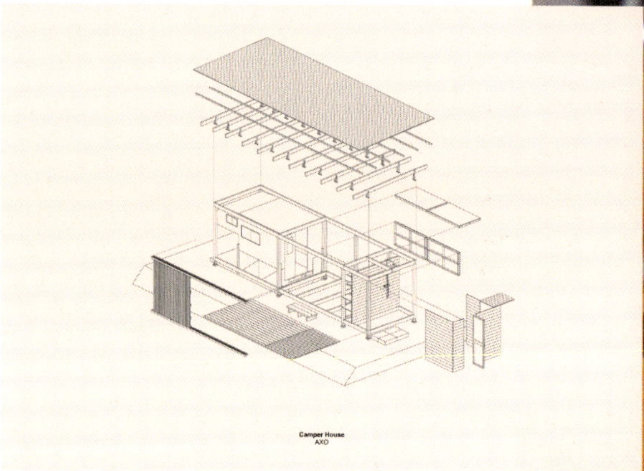

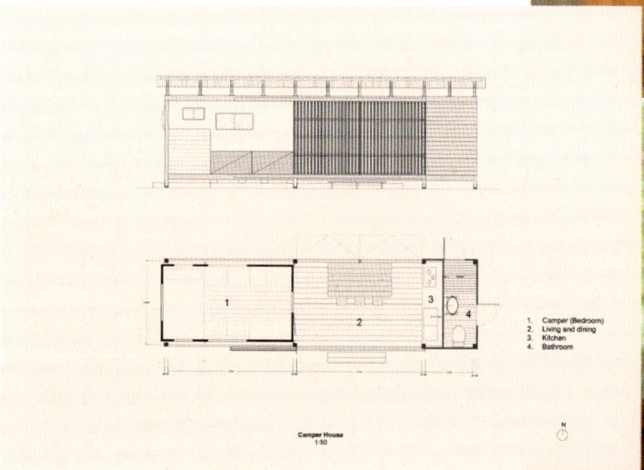

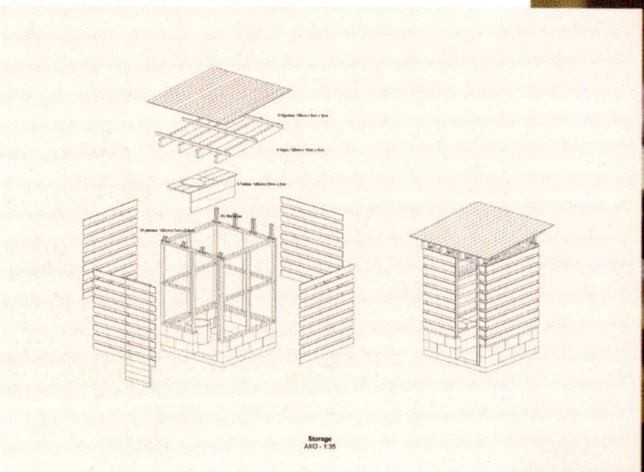

previous

The casual assembly of elements complements the camper that was its point of origin.

this page

Above, exploded axonometric drawings and a plan. Right, a hammock is strung near the opening in the kitchen space.

WOOD AND MOUNTAIN

Mae Rim, Chiang Mai, Thailand, 2021

SHER MAKER, *Chiang Mai*

WOOD AND MOUNTAIN is a 1,076-square-foot (100-square-meter) cabin. Recuperated wood and local (Mae Rim) tiles were used in the design. The wood was charred before being applied to a steel structure wall system that is frequently employed in northern Thailand. Burning the wood to make it more resistant is inspired by the traditional Japanese shou sugi ban technique. The architects explain, "This method was adapted to use characteristics of local Thai wood, which is more resistant to weather conditions" than most imported wood. The burning process itself was an important part of the design scheme. "Our intention was to carry out the expressive part of the architecture ourselves. We carried out the entire burning process in our workshop. Using wood burning for us is not just about seeking a kind of aesthetic statement, it is about understanding the material and making it by hand. Our idea was to leave the imperfections in each shade of burnt wooden plank to emphasize that this building is a work of architecture made by human hands, a human expression." The gridded steel structure, which is also blackened, gives a decidedly modern appearance to this modest house, but the overhanging roof and charred wood also make it blend into the forest setting and appear to be closely connected to this place. It suggests an interesting way to reconcile modernity and local traditions and content. The use of locally sourced wood and labor assures that the building is relatively respectful of environmental concerns despite the steel frame. Local climatic conditions make living at once indoors and outdoors practical. Built in a forested area, the structure has a bedroom, a living/pantry space, and a wooden deck. Thongchai Chansamak and Patcharada Inplang are "architects and makers." Chansamak was born in Udon Thani, Thailand, in 1990, and Inplang was born the same year in Lampang. They established Sher Maker in 2018.

left

A living space seen here opens entirely to a wooden deck, which has a hot tub. The full-height windows open entirely, making this interior space communicate fully with the outdoors.

following

Stairs lead up from the living space to a bedroom located just above. It also features full-height operable glazing along with dark wood floors and walls. Section drawings as well as lower and upper floor plans show the narrow rectangular form of the house.

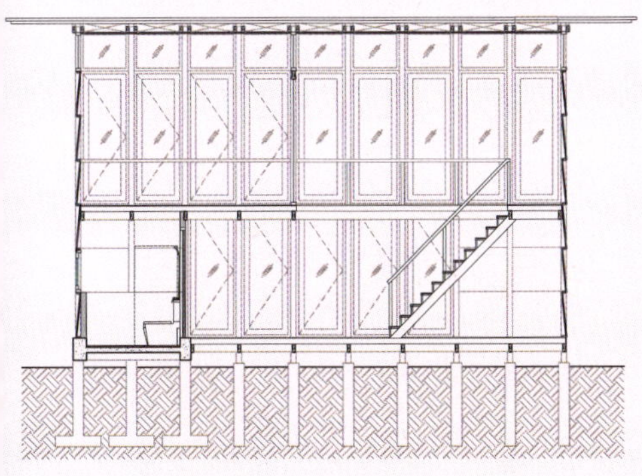

SECTION A

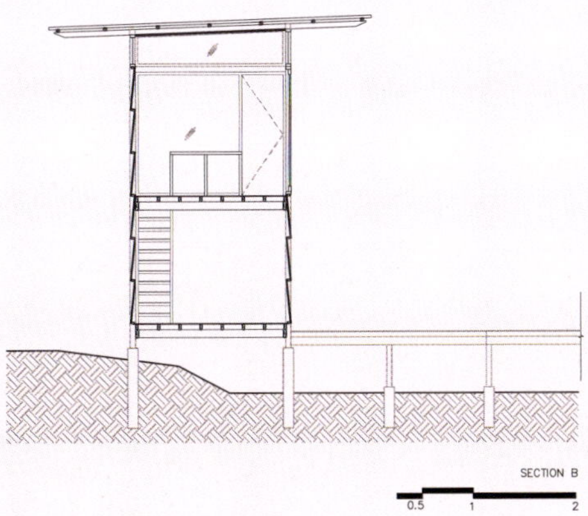

SECTION B

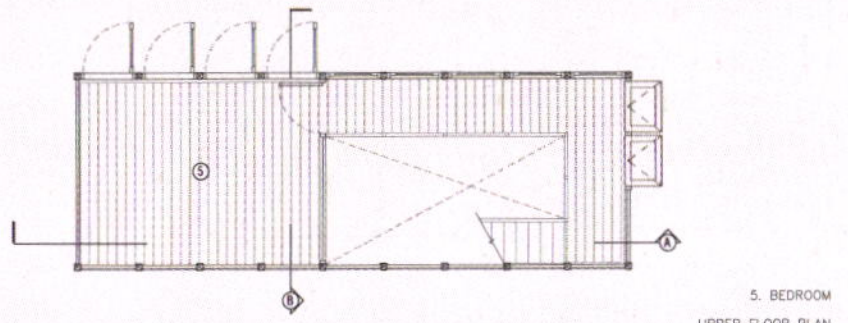

5. BEDROOM

UPPER FLOOR PLAN

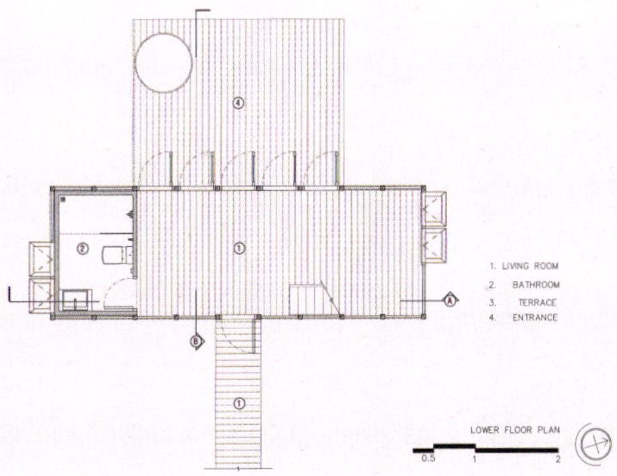

1. LIVING ROOM
2. BATHROOM
3. TERRACE
4. ENTRANCE

LOWER FLOOR PLAN

THE BOLDER

Lysefjorden, Norway, 2023

SNØHETTA, *Oslo*

IN A PROJECT CARRIED forward with a local entrepreneur (Tom Bjarte Norland), the large Oslo office Snøhetta designed four cabins on the western coast of Norway, near the Lysefjorden, about 46 miles (75 kilometers) east of Stavanger by road. The architects state that the cabins are lifted off the ground on concrete pillars and "designed to harmonize in the best possible way with the surrounding nature and blur the lines between being indoors and outdoors." Glass facades and skylights give residents unrivaled views of the natural setting and make them feel that they are "floating in the air." The interior design, with "natural and durable materials in earthy colors and organic textures" was selected to underline the connection to nature. The upper level of the cabins is equipped with a kitchen and dining space designed by Vipp, with whom the architects have worked in the past. The ground floors have a built-in bed and bathroom. The main materials used in the construction are untreated red cedar and concrete with aggregate from the site. The cabins are almost entirely off-grid and have naturally sourced spring water. The entire site is due for further construction in the future, to include a lounge and a gourmet restaurant serving "locally sourced" food. The Bolder succeeds in combining the architectural sophistication and expertise of Snøhetta with a natural site, providing a comfortable setting in a near-wilderness environment. The fact that the cabins are set up off the ground minimizes damage to the site while the off-grid aspect of the project also ensures that it has a relatively small carbon footprint and a good prospect for being considered a sustainable intervention.

left

The small wooden houses sit in the rocks above a breathtaking fjord landscape.

following

The interiors are designed to allow the residents to take in the views, almost as if they are outdoors in a protected place.

MUSUBI HOUSE

Paauilo, Hawaii, United States, 2020

CRAIG STEELY ARCHITECTURE, *San Francisco*

THE 100-ACRE (40-hectare) site of this house is on the northeast slope of Mauna Kea on the Big Island of Hawaii. Built with in-situ concrete, it employs photovoltaic panels and rooftop rainwater collection to remain entirely off-grid. The windy location is characterized by fields of wainaku (*Panicum repens*) grass. The client sought to embrace the environment of the site with its waves of windblown grass. The architects state, "We responded with a house that floats in this rolling sea of grass like a ship floats in the ocean. Like a ship's prow, the sharpest end of this triangular house deflects the formidable wind." As seen from a distance, the house appears to have a solid, flat roof that hovers over almost entirely glazed walls that allow residents to fully take in the view of the expansive natural setting. Craig Steely explains that the name of the house was derived from the shape of its plan, which looks like "the Hawaiian version of the Japanese wrapped rice snack onigiri." The scheme of the design is in fact based on outdoor and indoor triangles made with curving concrete walls—the indoor area including the bedrooms, kitchen, and the living/working area. The center of the 2,200-square-foot (204-square-meter) house is marked by a triangular courtyard with a floor paved in pahoehoe lava, originally formed by hot, fluid magma. The fully glazed interior can open almost entirely into this space. An outdoor shower is shielded by ferns and palms. The architect explains, "The clients' willingness to prioritize permeability over privacy gave us the freedom to create a plan without doors or hard boundaries. Spaces flow from zone to zone while always remaining in visual contact with the rolling landscape. Grass flows right up to the edge of the floor-to-ceiling glass walls. Looking out the windows onto the rolling grass landscape is like watching waves on the open sea." Based in both California and Hawaii, the architect Craig Steely is known for creating "unique hybrids of these two environments." He received his architecture degree from Cal Poly (San Luis Obispo).

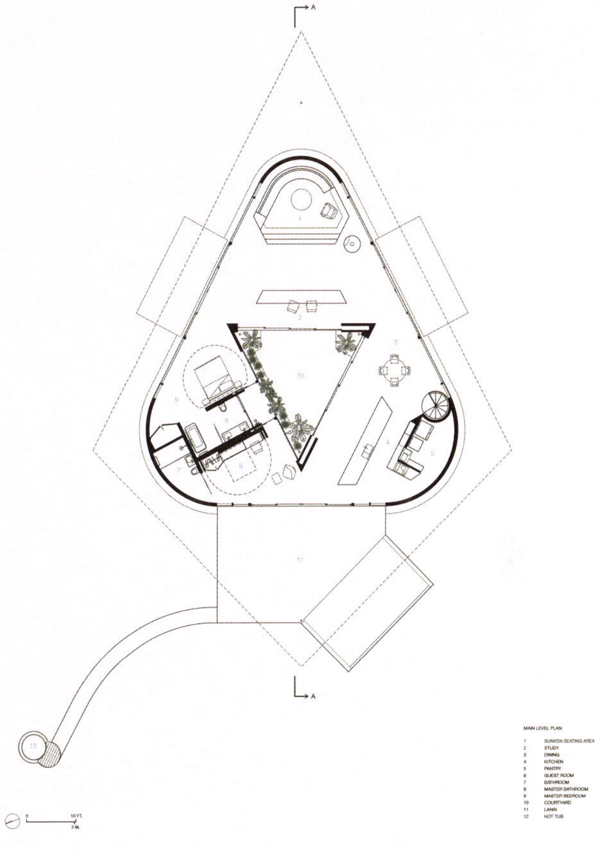

previous

The house is inserted into the landscape, lying low but still open to its environment.

above

Unusual triangular plan of the house with, left, its triangular inner courtyard.

following

The living room is sunken into its concrete environment, allowing for nearly uninterrupted views of the natural setting. A round skylight is placed above the bathroom.

AURORA LODGE

Lyngen, Norway, 2020

SNORRE STINESSEN ARCHITECTURE, *Tromsø*

THE AURORA LODGE IS IN northern Norway. It faces west toward the Norwegian Sea, which is part of the Arctic Ocean. All the trees on this wilderness site were preserved during construction, as were other parts of the natural vegetation on the site. It was built on a plot of private, protected land measuring just over 49 acres (20 hectares). The house has a concrete floor and terraces and is based on an A-frame design, which the architect has "tilted back" to provide better views, assured by the 16.4-foot (5-meter) ceilings and glass walls. The exterior cladding is in Nordic Green (pre-patinated) copper, and indoors silver fir (*Abies alba*) was used. The structure includes two units and a separate suite facing the sea. The wing on the south side has three bedrooms, a living room, and kitchen on the ground floor, and another two bedrooms in a loft space. The entrance and living room are on the north side. A central terrace takes the form of an interior courtyard with a fireplace suspended from the roof. A communal kitchen and dining room are in the northern part of the building, which also has views of the water. A separate suite with kitchen and bathroom is in an annex. A sauna, clad in copper like the house, also opens to the ocean. The architect states, "The positioning of the buildings follows the natural formation of the terrain. The concrete for the floors was sourced locally. The copper was chosen for its longevity in the seaside climate and is a material found naturally in all living organisms. The complete construction follows the principles of healthy living, with materials specifically chosen to avoid toxic substances in the interior air. The building is, of course, extremely well insulated (we are in the Arctic North), but construction here is based on the principles of naturally breathing of materials—similar to a traditional log building. The buildings have a positive carbon footprint. All exterior stone is sourced locally. All wood is of the highest European standards, ecologically and sustainably sourced and machined. The buildings are connected to the local hydropower grid but are prepared for planned electrical independence within three to five years." Snorre Stinessen was born in 1974 in Tromsø, northern Norway, where his firm is located today. He received his degrees in architecture from the Norwegian Institute of Technology in Trondheim and the Polytechnic University of Milan (1999). Lyngen, where the Aurora Lodge is located, is about 43 miles (69 kilometers) east of Tromsø.

left

A narrow platform sitting above the ground is protected by the extended eaves of the house.

opposite

The pre-patinated green copper of the exterior is visible near courtyard space opening to the living area.

byStinessen

NEST HOUSE

Herefordshire, UK, 2021

STUDIO BARK, *London*

THE NEST HOUSE WAS BUILT using a modular and demountable non-profit construction system called U-Build. The retired couple who were the clients for the Nest House wanted "an environmentally responsible design that would cater to their long-term physical needs, due to disability." The structure was built in the summer of 2021 by a dozen students from across the UK to involve them actively in a "rigorously sustainable design." Arranged around a central courtyard, the house was built without any concrete or structural steel. The foundation is reusable and has timber floor and roof beams. The project includes a green roof and a planted trellis. The construction system provided for plywood parts to be brought to the site in flat packs. A system that carefully accounts for embodied carbon was used to assure the most efficient design possible. Studio Bark explains, "The project's embodied and operational carbon counts are notably low due to fabric first principles, local and natural materials used, high levels of zero-waste insulation and airtightness, on-site renewables, and [the] 'smart' infrared heating system." Electricity is provided by photovoltaic panels, batteries, and Graphene sheet infrared heating panels. Insulation is sheep's wool from the UK, and the building system required no use of heavy lifting equipment. The area around the house was planted with wildflowers and an orchard. Gracious, one of the students involved in the project, stated, "Since completing my part 1 in the peak of the pandemic, an opportunity like this to get out there and be hands-on with architecture and to see how everything translates from paper to real life, especially with such a supportive group of people, has been a lovely experience which has affected what I think architecture is and what role I want to play. [. . . I] hope that programs like this [can] hopefully someday be implemented in the education system." The house offers an area of 1,367 square feet (127 square meters) and was built for a cost of £280,000 (about 357,000 USD).

opposite

The simple, covered wooden terrace of the house allows residents to take in the surroundings.

right

Interiors of the house are almost entirely clad in wood, giving a warm feeling that does not necessarily impose a feeling of radical sustainability.

DIMENSIONS X OM1

Krinklewood Vineyard, Broke, New South Wales, Australia, 2022

PETER STUTCHBURY ARCHITECTURE (PSA), *Newport, New South Wales*

PETER STUTCHBURY SET OUT to "launch a planet-friendly base model housing unit that represents current technologies and responsibilities." OM1 can be erected in a period of six weeks and is "cost-effective and recyclable." A flexible skylight system helps to reduce any requirement for energy. Set up off the ground on *pilotis*, or pillars, the house has a total floor area of 613 square feet (57 square meters) but can be readily changed in size using the modular system. OM1 will be available in four sizes ranging from 161 to 646 square feet (15 to 60 square meters) internally, but each design is flexible with no set layout. There is an outdoor stone terrace on one side of this house, and a wooden one with a bathtub on the other side, which, like the house itself, is lifted off the ground and is concrete-free. The principal in charge of this project (and the photographer who took these images) was Alejo Achaval. Wood is used extensively for floors, ceilings, and walls. Cross-laminated timber (CLT) was used for the structure. Sliding glass windows allow the interior to be opened almost entirely, and a wood-burning stove can provide heat. The house has something of a handmade feeling about it, and yet it is designed, as the architect emphasizes, according to current technical standards. The project was developed with the Australian entrepreneur Oscar Martin. This first model was built at Krinklewood Vineyard, which also belongs to Martin. Stutchbury was born in 1954 and lived "on the land" as a child, with aborigines on the banks of the Darling River and with tribes in the highlands of New Guinea. Since 1995, his firm, PSA, has won sixty-two Royal Australian Institute of Architects Awards. Stutchbury was the 2015 winner of the Gold Medal of the Australian Institute of Architects.

right

Elevation drawings and a site plan reveal the rectangular form of the house and the way that it is in good part lifted off the ground.

below and opposite

The house seen inside and in a partial exterior view gives a distinctive impression of light, simple design.

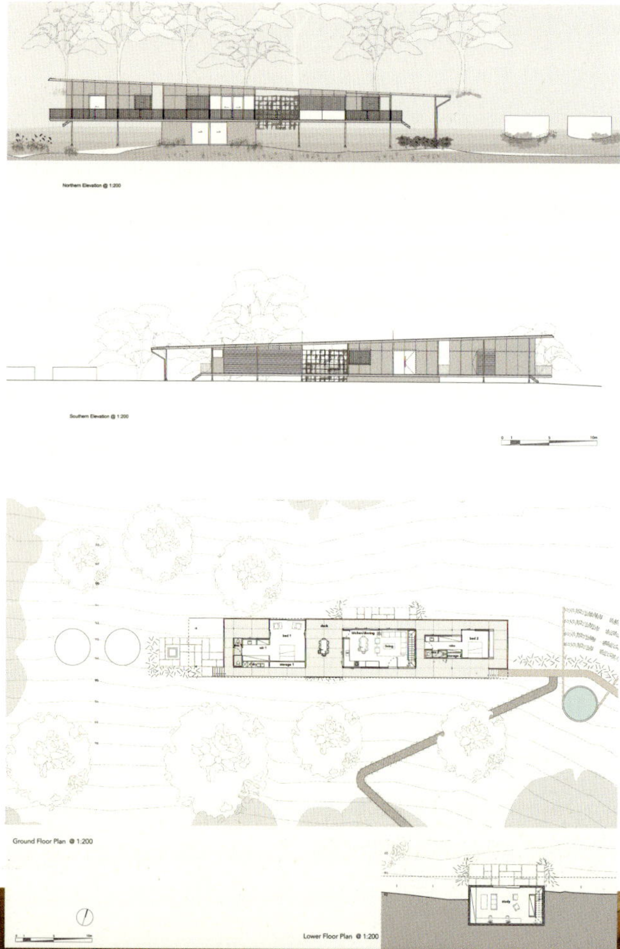

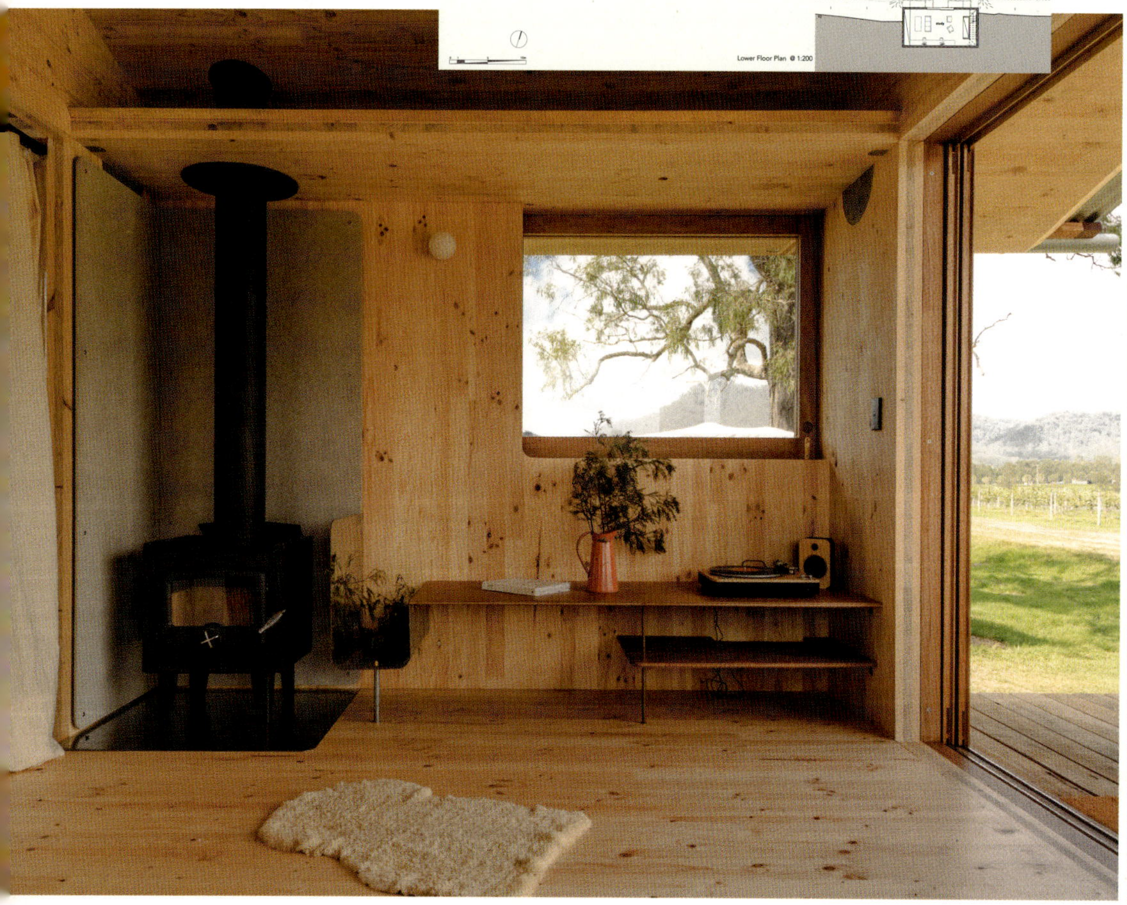

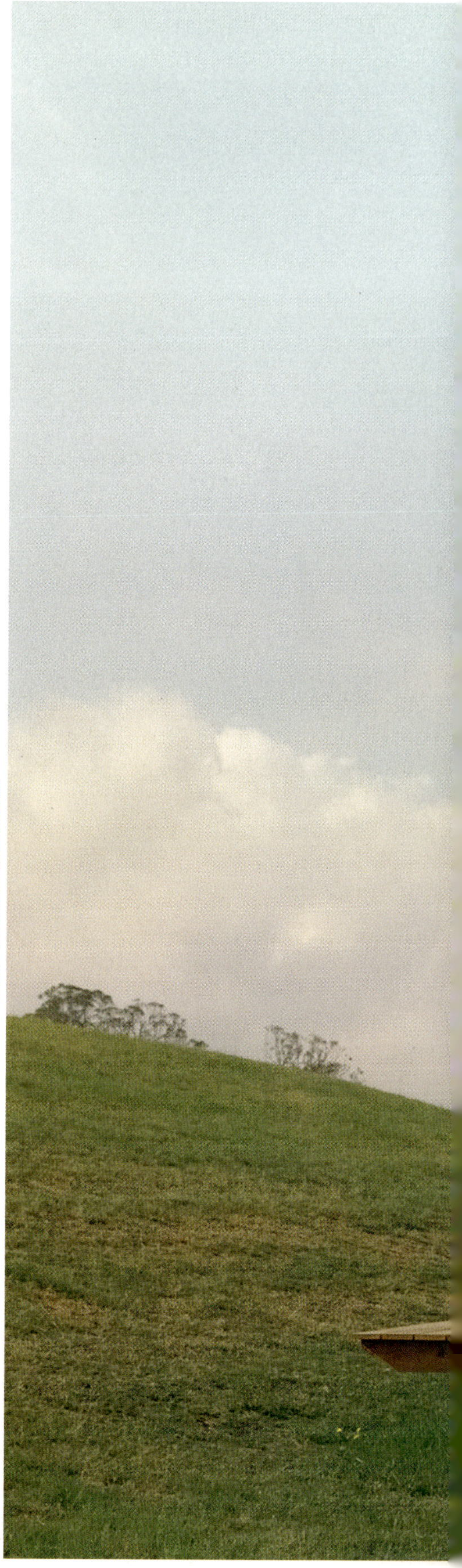

UPSIDE DOWN AKUBRA HOUSE

Nundle, New South Wales, Australia, 2019

ALEXANDER SYMES ARCHITECT,
Camperdown, New South Wales

THE ARCHITECTS EXPLAIN that the form of this off-grid house located in a bull paddock was inspired by the Australian Akubra hat. Created in 1911 by Benjamin Dunkerley in Surry Hills (Sydney), the hat remains a strong symbol of the country. The large roof of this house can be imagined as the broad brim of the hat. The 6,027-square-foot (560-square-meter) roof, which is two and a half times larger than the building footprint, is intended to block out all summer sun, yet allow in the winter sun to warm the central spine of the home as well as collect rainwater to run the house. A 28,266-gallon (107,000-liter) water storage tank is part of the scheme. The house has a service core at its center and living spaces around the perimeter. The kitchen and living space open toward Hanging Rock, a place where gold was found in the 1850s. The 861-square-foot (80-square-meter) carport is covered with photovoltaic panels (LG NeON H BiFacial) "celebrating the technology that powers the whole house." Integrated into clear glass modules, these photovoltaics allow filtered daylight into the carport. The interior of the house offers views of Hanging Rock through 10-foot-high (3-meter) blackbutt double-glazed sliding doors. Bedrooms, with window area limited to reduce solar gain, are in the west wing of the house. Utility and service rooms are in the central spine, which is marked by an off-form concrete wall. The architect Alexander Symes explains, "The home is influenced by simple practical rural buildings which inform its metal, timber, and concrete material palette, responding to the client's brief for a robust and practical house." Symes graduated from the University of New South Wales in 2006 and founded his firm in 2014. The house is in Nundle, which is 244 miles (392 kilometers) north of Sydney and 42 miles (68 kilometers) south of Tamworth. Built on a large 158-acre (64-hectare) site, the house offers 2,045 square feet (190 square meters) of floor space.

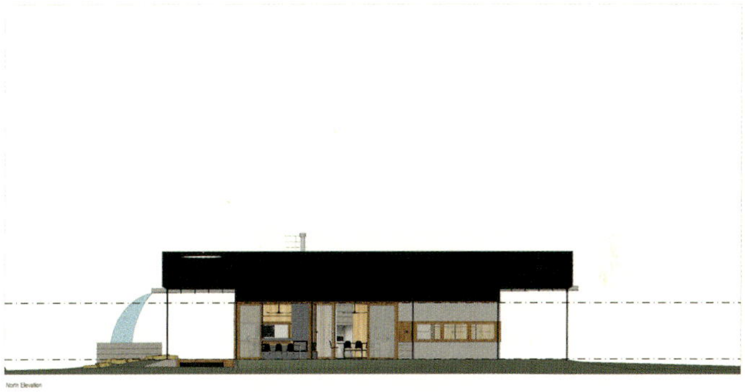

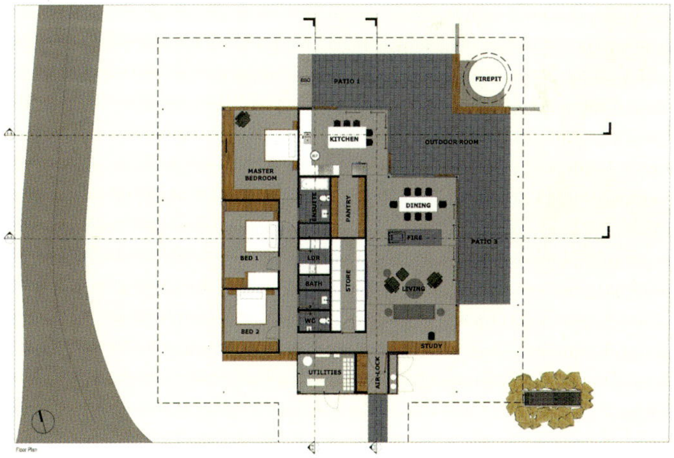

left

Sliding walls open the house entirely to its stone-clad patio.

above

Elevation and plan drawings.

JOSHUA TREE CASE STUDY CABIN

Joshua Tree, California, United States, 2017

MIKE VENSEL, *Los Angeles*

THIS PROJECT IS PARTICULARLY unusual in that its creator is not an architect as such, but instead, an "artist, designer, and photographer." Mike Vensel has been involved in fashion but also in the creation of "case study cabins." In this case, he explains, "The Joshua Tree Case Study Cabin explores the ways in which architecture can disappear into the landscape when not in use. Using simple materials such as lightweight waterproof fabric and pressure-treated lumber, the shell of the cabin can be removed and the frame can fold flat when not in use. All of the furniture along with the fabric shell can be stored and secured underneath the floor. The cabin is completely off the grid with solar power, rainwater capture, and a composting toilet." The very ephemeral structure measures 8 by 26 feet, or 208 square feet (2.4 by 7.9 meters, or 19 square meters). The Case Study Cabins are designed specifically with the environment in mind and hand-built by Vensel with "minimal material and tools as an experiment to see how simply we can build/live." Vensel suggests that such designs could be an inspiration for ways to give homeless people in California an inexpensive solution to their problems. The designs are inspired by nomadic peoples such as North American Indians and Mongolians but created using modern building techniques for costs under $2,000 per project. Another project by Vensel involves a larger 400-square-foot (37-square-meter) house with solid sides and glass doors "inspired by Wright's Fallingwater and by Mies van der Rohe's Farnsworth House." Vensel is an American artist whose works explore ideas of "simplicity, structure, fluidity, nature, and form" in various media including painting, drawing, sculpture, photography, video art, digital art, performance art, and fashion design.

TROPIK WORKS

Playa Grande, Guanacaste, Costa Rica, 2016

VOID, *San José*

ACCORDING TO THE ARCHITECTS, this was the first (modern) off-grid residence in Costa Rica. The country has engaged in various efforts to become carbon neutral, and to fully decarbonize by 2050. Noting that construction is one of the most significant contributors to CO_2 emissions, the architects explain, "We have based ourselves on three fundamental principles: efficiency, double functionality, and maintaining a closed cycle, where each of these principles is materialized in the architecture." The efficiency of construction was achieved using a pre-fabrication system that allowed the house to be assembled on-site. The structure is lifted up off the ground on thin pillars for a minimal impact on the site. The architects state, "Double functionality is achieved because the architecture is conceived to fulfill and resolve a specific climatic parameter." Cross ventilation and an elevated central patio "define the unit as a living component that breathes from its interior." The house takes advantage of air currents and thermal variations in a passive way, and rainwater is used for food production on-site. Solar panels are incorporated into the design, and Tropik Works thus was created as a "100% sustainable off-grid system." The floor area of the house, located on the Northern Pacific Coast of Costa Rica, is 2,315 square feet (215 square meters). Making broad use of wood for the terrace, some walls and sunscreens, Tropik Works is a modern take on sustainability, not projecting the "self-made" image of some off-grid houses but instead seeking to be resolutely modern and comfortable. VOID is an architecture firm founded in 2012 in Costa Rica by Sergio Frugone, Felipe Rossi, and Ricardo Sevilla.

left

A sunscreen shelters this outside terrace also seen from the exterior on the right.

opposite

The screens can be drawn aside according to the angle of the sun. The house is set off the ground on relatively light pillars.

CAPTAIN KELLY'S COTTAGE

Bruny Island, Tasmania, Australia, 2016

JOHN WARDLE, *Melbourne*

THE ARCHITECT RESTORED an 1840s cottage on the site, which had been altered over the course of one hundred seventy-five years. "Unsympathetic" alterations to the house were removed, and it was "made responsive to today's inhabitation standards." Bruny Island is located off the southeastern coast of Tasmania. It was originally inhabited by Aboriginal Tasmanians and was visited by James Cook in 1777. The island was named after the French explorer Bruni d'Entrecasteaux, who discovered that the land mass was an island in 1792. This 3,444-square-foot (320-square-meter) house is situated on a very large 1,087-acre (440-hectare) site located on a remote bay. The architect indicates that a new living area was added between the existing kitchen and bedrooms. Tasmanian oak (a type of eucalyptus) was used throughout the house. The original veranda "extends and encapsulates the new works, tying new and old together. This is reflected both in plan and section." A new chimney was added where there had been one in the past, and a north-facing courtyard was created on the leeward (i.e., facing away from prevailing winds) side of the structure. The courtyard was placed around one-hundred-year-old walnut and mulberry trees. The architect explains, "This reinstatement of the chimney helps to define and warm the courtyard space and is constructed of prototyped custom made white 'ghost' bricks." John Wardle received his bachelor's degree in architecture from RMIT University (Melbourne, 1980). He did postgraduate studies at Burnley Horticultural College (Melbourne, 1983) and obtained his master's degree in architecture from RMIT in 2001. Wardle was the winner of the 2020 Australian Institute of Architects Gold Medal. The jury citation read in part, "John Wardle is an architect's architect. He is a designer of consummate skill, whose works, from the smallest intricate piece of joinery to complex high-rise buildings, receive detailed attention and conscientious formal experiment."

MIND YOUR HEAD

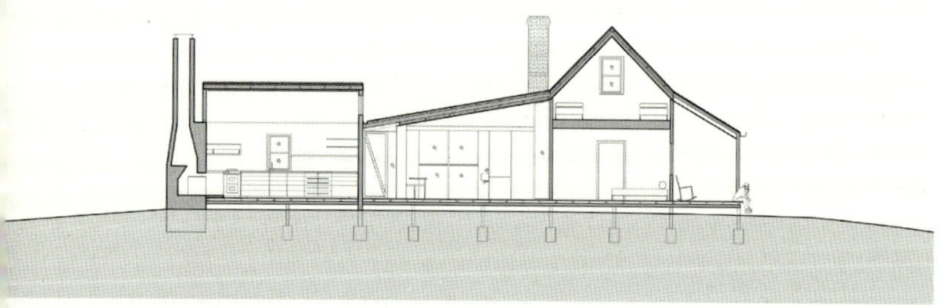

Section

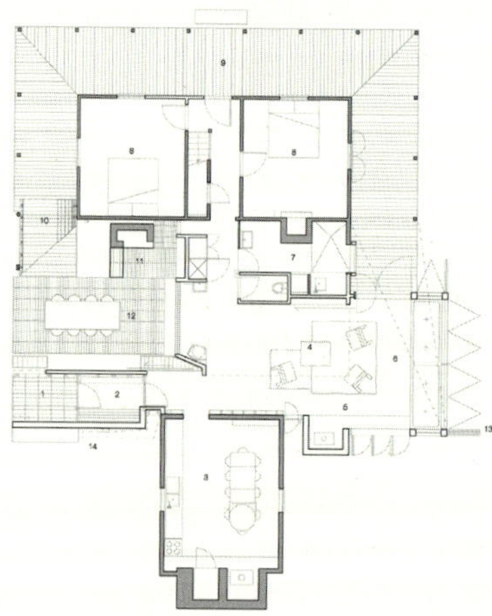

Ground Floor Plan

KEY LEGEND

1. Entry
2. Boot Room
3. Kitchen
4. Living
5. Fireplace Seat
6. Window Seat
7. Bathroom
8. Bedroom
9. Verandah
10. Reading Seat
11. External Fireplace
12. Courtyard
13. Operable Shutters
14. Lunch Bell

previous

The simple brick and wood design includes a wood-burning oven. A section drawing and a plan reveal the overall forms of the house.

left

A sliding glass door and an elevated platform allow residents to open the space to the outside, in a space filled with natural light.

RECREATION HOUSE

Utrecht, The Netherlands, 2014

ZECC ARCHITECTEN, *Utrecht*

REALIZED IN COLLABORATION with the designer Roel van Norel, this small house was built in a rural area at the edge of a forest to the north of Utrecht. The fully glazed west façade with moveable window shutters faces a garden. With the shutters in the open position, the interior of the house appears to be almost entirely open to the garden. Built on the site of a former garden house, the new structure reuses the existing foundation, which thus also determined its rectangular form. The architects employed what they call an "archetypal cottage" design with a slate gable roof and Western cedar (*Thuja plicata*) cladding. The careful design of the house includes all interior details. The front of the house includes a kitchen/dining/living area, with a bed to the rear and a small mezzanine level above that can be reached by climbing a ladder. Spaces can be divided or opened using sliding panels. The kitchen, toilet, shower, sink, and storage cabinets are located near the closed side of the house, along with a wood-burning stove. The architects emphasize that "even the plinth of the kitchen was designed as a drawer . . . every square inch of the house is used and thought-out." This design of course uses a standard A-frame form, but its broad expanse of glazing and its modern finishing give it a very contemporary and "architectural" feeling. It is open to the natural setting and designed to be able to reduce solar gain. It makes ample use of natural materials (wood and slate in particular). Zecc Architecten was created in Utrecht in 2003 by Rolf Bruggink and Marnix van der Meer. Van der Meer is still a partner in the firm, as is Bart Kellerhuis, who is currently the creative director.

Photo Credits

Cover, pp. 88–89, 90–91, 92 top, 92 bottom, 93 top, 93 bottom: Photographs by Boys Place Nice

pp. 1, 248–49, 250–51, 251 top right, 251 bottom right, 252 top, 252 bottom, 253: Courtesy Snøhetta, Oslo

pp. 2–3, 150–51, 152–53: Photographs by Anna Positano

pp. 5, 24–25, 263, 264, 265, 266, 267 top, 267 bottom: Photographs by Melissa Hegge

pp. 6, 224–25, 226–27, 227 right, 228–29: Photographs by Filippo Simonetti

pp. 8, 186–87, 188, 189, 190 top left, 190 center left, 190 bottom left, 190–91: Photographs by Nic Lehoux

pp. 11, 292–93, 294, 295 top, 295 bottom, 296, 297, 298–99: Photographs by Trevor Mein

pp. 12, 78–79, 80–81, 82–83, 196–97, 198, 199 top, 199 bottom, 200 top, 200 bottom, 201, 212–13, 214 left, 214–15, 216 top, 216 bottom, 217 top, 217 bottom: Photographs by Sandra Pereznieto

pp. 15, 105, 106–7, 108, 109 top, 109 bottom, 168–69, 170 top, 170 bottom, 171 top, 171 bottom, 172 top, 172 bottom, 173: Photographs by Cristobal Palma, Estudio Palma

pp. 16–17, 26–27, 28, 29, 30, 31 top, 31 bottom: Photographs by Andrey Avdeenko

pp. 19, 73, 74, 75 top, 75 bottom, 76, 77: Courtesy Florian Busch Architects, Tokyo

pp. 20, 202–3, 204 top, 204 bottom, 205 top, 205 bottom: Courtesy Michael Quirk Design, Boulder, Colorado

pp. 23, 95, 96 top, 96 bottom, 97 top, 97 bottom, 134–35, 136 left, 136–37, 138 top, 138 bottom, 139, 192–93, 194 top, 194 bottom, 195, 218–19, 220 top, 220 bottom, 221, 222–23: Photographs by James Silverman

pp. 32–33, 34–35, 35 bottom, 36 top, 36 bottom, 37: Photographs by Nin Solis

pp. 39, 40 right, 41, 42, 43: Photographs by Rory Gardiner

pp. 44–45, 46, 47 top, 47 bottom, 48 top left, 48 center left, 48 bottom left, 48–49: Photographs by Leo Finotti

pp. 50–51, 52–53, 54–55, 56–57, 57 right: Photographs by Joana França

pp. 58, 60, 61, 62, 63: Photographs by Amy Barkow

pp. 65, 66–67, 67 top: Photographs by William Abranowicz

pp. 68–69, 70 top, 70 bottom, 71 top, 71 bottom left, 71 bottom right: Photographs by Caroline Kite

pp. 84–85, 86 top, 86 bottom, 87 top, 87 bottom: Photographs by Trent Bell

pp. 98–99, 100 left, 100–101, 102, 103: Photographs by Earl Carter

pp. 110–11, 112, 113: Courtesy Hebra Arquitectos, Vitacura

pp. 114–15, 116–17, 117 top right, 117 center right, 117 bottom right: Photographs by José Hevia

pp. 118–19, 120 top, 120 bottom, 120–21, 122 top, 122 bottom, 123 top, 123 bottom: Courtesy Hollaway Studio, London

pp. 124–25, 126 top left, 126 bottom left, 126–27, 174–75, 176–77, 177 top right, 177 center right, 177 bottom right, 178 top, 178 bottom, 179: Photographs by Roland Halbe

pp. 128–29, 130 bottom left, 130–31, 131 top, 132–133: Courtesy Jacobschang, New York

pp. 140–41, 142–43, 143 top right, 143 center right, 143 bottom right: Courtesy Tom Kundig – Olson Kundig Architects, Seattle

pp. 144–45, 146, 147, 148–49: Photographs by Chikako Harada

pp. 154–55, 156 top, 156 bottom, 157 top, 157 bottom: Photographs by Jo Smith

pp. 158–59, 160, 161 top, 161 bottom: Courtesy Material Cultures, London

pp. 162–63, 164–65, 165 right, 166 top, 166 bottom, 167 top, 167 bottom: Photographs by Blue Sky / Mariashot

pp. 180–81, 182 top left, 182 center left, 182 bottom left, 182–83, 184 top, 184 bottom, 185 top: Courtesy Shinichi Ogawa & Associates, Hiroshima / Tokyo

pp. 206–7, 208–9, 210 top, 210 bottom, 211: Photographs by Jag Studio

pp. 230–31, 232, 233, 234 left, 234–35: Photographs by Thomas Jantscher

pp. 236–37, 238 left, 238–39, 240–41: Courtesy Daniel Serrano, Chinandega, Nicaragua

pp. 242–43, 244–45, 246 left, 246–47: Courtesy Sher Maker, Chiang Mai

pp. 254–55, 256 top left, 256 center left, 256 bottom left, 256–57, 258–29, 260 top left, 260 bottom left, 260–61: Courtesy Craig Steely Architecture, San Francisco

pp. 268–69, 270, 271 top, 271 bottom: Photographs by Andy Billman

pp. 272–73, 274 left, 274–75: Photographs by Alejo Achaval

pp. 276–77, 278, 279, 280–81: Photographs by Barton Taylor

pp. 282–83, 284–85: Courtesy Mike Vensel, Los Angeles

pp. 286–87, 288, 289 top, 289 bottom, 290 top, 290 bottom, 291 top, 291 bottom: Photographs by Andres Garcia Lachner

pp. 300–301, 302, 303 top, 303 bottom: Photographs by Stijn Poelstra

First published in the United States of America in 2024 by
Rizzoli International Publications, Inc.
300 Park Avenue South
New York, NY 10010
www.rizzoliusa.com

Text **PHILIP JODIDIO**

Publisher **CHARLES MIERS**
Editor **ELLEN R. COHEN**
Managing Editor **LYNN SCRABIS**
Production Manager **KAIJA MARKOE**

Design **SARAH GIFFORD**

2024 2025 2026 2027 2028 / 10 9 8 7 6 5 4 3 2 1

ISBN: 978-0-8478-3431-0
Library of Congress Control Number: 2024934579

PRINTED IN CHINA

MIX Paper | Supporting responsible forestry FSC™ C005748

p. 1

The Bolder, Snøhetta

pp. 2–3

The Hermitage, LLABB

p. 5

Aurora Lodge, Snorre Stinessen Architecture

p. 6

Rifugio, Hans-Jörg Ruch